HYPER-CONNECTED SELLING

Winning More Business by Leveraging Digital Influence and Creating Human Connection

DAVID J.P. FISHER

Contents

PART II: THE OLD SCHOOL IS THE NEW SCHOOL

PART III: WORKING THE NETWORKING

Introduction

When I first told my friend Ian about this book, he had a quizzical look for the first minute or two, then stopped me and said, "Oh! You're not telling people how to *get* hyper-connected. You're telling them what to do because the world already *is* hyper-connected. Got it!"

The light bulb that went off for Ian is the same one I want to spark in your mind. Learning how to be Hyper-Connected is like learning how to read critically. You already know how to read, just like you already know how to sell, but you can take it to the next level by being intentional with what you're doing. Your work in the modern sales world would benefit hugely from deliberate development.

During the past two decades, I've helped thousands of professionals connect more effectively, whether through offline networking, social selling, or building relationships with sales prospects. In these years, the world has changed quite a bit. Reaching out to new sales prospects used to take most of a salesperson's time and attention. This was the world of cold calls and door-to-door sales, and those who excelled at those skills stood out as the rain-makers who brought in the business. They were the salespeople who won all the sales contests and commanded the big commissions in the sexiest industries. Having a lot of connections used to be impressive. Not anymore.

These days, having connections isn't that big of a deal. It's almost a given. Technology means that we're only an email, tweet, or text away from most people, and along with that comes a never-ending stream of content: messages, videos, pictures, and more. Information used to be a scarce resource; now it's a commodity in such impressive supply that it threatens to drown us.

I call this the Hyper-Connected world: one in which people, information, and places are connected like never before, and one that has massively changed how sales professionals go about their jobs. We're being forced to change, but not because something changed in how we sell—rather, it's because the Hyper-Connected world has profoundly changed *how people buy*. The ways that customers go about purchasing products and services are shifting rapidly. To stay relevant (and employed), sales professionals have to find new ways to bring value to the people they serve. If they can't, they'll quickly go the way of the dodo.

Today's Sales Sherpa™

How does a sales professional provide value in a Hyper-Connected world? That's the question this book seeks to definitely answer, and the first place to look is *how salespeople gather and share information*. In the past, salespeople provided value by being the sole source of the information their prospects needed to make buying decisions. They were the direct conduit between the prospect and the prospect's solutions. Most salespeople served transactional roles, providing information about the product and then taking the order.

Today, it's no longer enough to be the information-provider and order-taker. These roles are being outsourced to websites, mobile apps, or robots. Information in and of itself is just a commodity these days, and when a product or service becomes a commodity, its value plummets, and there is little marginal value left. Considering that internet traffic hit the one zettabyte mark in 2016 (that's one thousand billion billion bytes), we can be confident that information on its own doesn't have much value.[1]

Customers once lacked information, but now, they have too much. What they need is someone who can help them process and interpret the overwhelming amount of information they do have. They're looking for someone who can guide them through the decision-making process, helping them translate the information they have into a usable form that they can use to make a better decision.

I call this new type of salesperson a Sales Sherpa™. This term is inspired by the Sherpa people in Nepal, who guide travelers through the unpredictable and sometimes treacherous pathways of the Himalayan mountains. Likewise, a Sales Sherpa guides prospects through the overwhelming and oftentimes confusing process of modern-day buying. Today's prospects are desperately seeking those who can help them make sense of a noisy, busy world. Whether you're selling directly to consumers or to businesses, the modern buyer has a

> **A Sales Sherpa guides prospects through the overwhelming and oftentimes confusing process of modern-day buying.**

wide landscape of information to contend with. They face decision-making processes that are more complicated than ever, and the sales professional who can skillfully hold their hand through it all will be in high demand.

The skillsets of the Sales Sherpa are different than some of the older selling techniques. Sales professionals can no longer try to force people into the simple, linear sales processes of the past that focused on making as many sales as possible, as fast as possible. In this complex, interconnected world, there are multiple steps that weave together to define the sales process. I call this new process a Sales Matrix™, because it's a wide, interconnected web that constitutes the context of the sale. In the past, sales professionals, and especially sales leadership, wanted an easy-to-follow formula to define sales activities. But more and more, selling is moving beyond the realm of simple equations. It's no longer about "hammering the phone" and finding tricks to "handle objections" to win the "numbers game." It's about engaging your prospects and customers while they're on their own complex buying journey.

The sales process is evolving, but it's not dying. A lot of people think that technology is the death knell of the sales profession, but they're wrong. True, technology is moving forward at breakneck speed, and transactional sales are moving online and being automated. But the complexity of sales decisions and human interaction means that we're not going to become pod people talking through fiber-optic cables any time soon. The relationships you build with your prospects and clients still have value. Whether you're selling real estate, software, or machine parts, the person across the table from you will seek your human connection and expertise. As the author Bryan Kramer says, "There is no more B2B or B2C sales anymore...it's H2H: Human to Human."[2]

> This is a book about the whys and hows of developing human-to-human sales relationships in the twenty-first century.

And therein lies the key: Successful sales professionals will harness technology to work for them, but the human element is going to remain central. Technology will be there to help us develop more, better, and stronger relationships.

This is a book about the whys and hows of developing human-to-human sales relationships in the twenty-first century. Sometimes those relationships will play out offline and sometimes online, but they will always require a solid grasp of interpersonal communication skills. This book will help you take everything you've learned about selling up to this point, then translate it for a new world. The skills and habits that propelled previous generations to success aren't going to cut it anymore, but they don't need to be abandoned. They just need to be updated.

Embracing the Complexity

When I was in grade school, I had a role in *The Music Man*, a musical that tells the story of a traveling huckster in the Iowa of 1912. Because I was still young, I got to play a shirt-tailed kid who eventually played the triangle in the town marching band. (Alas, Broadway stardom eluded me.) The story is full of interesting sales anecdotes, but the scene that sticks in my mind, even to this day, is the first one: A group of traveling salesmen rides a train to Iowa, gossiping about the scam artist Harold Hill. The salesman leading the pack in these complaints is an anvil salesman—I think the writer made him an anvil salesman to contrast him with the slickness of Harold Hill. Back then, selling anvils struck me as an odd, yet somewhat magical, profession.

Sometimes I think it would be simpler to go back to the turn of the twentieth century. I would hop on a train, travel to a new town, call on every blacksmith, sell a few anvils, then move on. I'm sure it was lonely on the road—you'd probably get tired of the train, and you'd keep hearing rumors about this horseless carriage thing that someone had invented. But still, life would be good. It's easy to romanticize. I wouldn't have to worry about checking my cell phone for texts, sending a tweet to a prospect, or polishing my LinkedIn profile. That is, until that rumored horseless carriage completely destroyed the blacksmith industry and with it, the need for my anvils.

Maybe life wasn't actually so simple back then. It definitely isn't now.

If you're hoping to find simple answers about the new sales landscape, you'll end up disappointed. You'll be right back here at the beginning, because those simple answers are more and more out of touch with what's really happening. The world has been evolving at a rapid pace over the past few decades, and if it's even possible, that change seems to be speeding up. The sales masters and ideas that came into their own in the last century are showing their age. Heck, the ideas that came out five years ago can be just as outdated.

Complexity is the new normal. We don't have to go back a hundred years to find a different world; we only have to go back a decade or two. In fact, it's likely that the world of ten years from now will be barely recognizable to us. New technologies have fundamentally altered how we work, live, and interact. In a world where every other article on LinkedIn seems to promise the secret to business success, it can be easy to get trapped into thinking that there's a simple way out. If that's what you want, those articles are out there. You can find them easily with a quick Google search. Unfortunately, these only offer you a quick band-aid to fit over just a small piece of your business problems.

> **Complexity is the new normal.**

Now is the time to develop your ability to embrace the change, leverage strategic thinking, and use a little creativity to drive your success. By the end of this book, you will be able to make informed, strategic decisions about how to spend your time and energy. Technology is taking over activities that don't require the depth of human thought and creativity, so it's more important than ever to embrace the skills that technology can't replace. Surprisingly, amid this complex information age, many old-school techniques in human-to-human interaction are becoming more important than ever.

The changing landscape of twenty-first century selling enables sales professionals to harness the power of old-school communication skills, networking, and social selling to win more business. The future, and by extension the present, belongs to professionals who understand how to leverage technology to enhance age-old communication skills. My goal is to give you the understanding, the strategies, and the tactics to make it happen. If you're reading this book, you came to it wanting to build your professional acumen and increase your productivity as a sales professional. I promise that I won't leave you hanging.

This book is divided into three parts. In the first, we look at how selling has evolved into its current state. We look at how the process of buying goods and products has changed over time, then examine how salespeople can organically integrate themselves

> **The future, and by extension the present, belongs to professionals who understand how to leverage technology to enhance age-old communication skills.**

into today's new buying process. In Part II, we will examine how the linear sales process has been replaced by a complex, three-dimensional landscape. We will review old-school interpersonal communication skills and show that these are key to traversing this new sales landscape. I will also show that building trust and interpersonal relationships is just as important on digital social media platforms. We break down the three key areas that the modern sales professional can leverage for greater results: old-school sales and interpersonal skills, networking, and social selling.

In Part III, we will see how these three areas combine to build a powerful sales program that allows for unprecedented types of social networking. Each of these sections will include a variety of examples and stories that will help you connect the strategies of Hyper-Connected selling to your daily selling activities. For additional resources, you can visit this book's webpage at hyperconnectedselling.com, where you will find information about the latest ideas coming out of the sales world, along with links to blogs, websites, and online groups. Whether you're looking for a way to construct the perfect LinkedIn profile, clues to conducting more effective sales calls in the Sales Matrix, or strategies for obtaining more referrals, we have you covered.

Before we get started on our journey through the past, present, and future of sales, I have a word of advice. In one of the many sales meetings I attended as a sales representative, a trainer once said, "Unused information is the same as ignorance." If you read through this book and then don't change your sales behaviors or activities, then you've wasted your time—and time is a very precious resource. As you read, I hope you will continuously ask yourself, "How can I apply this information to my daily work world?" If you approach this book with an open mind and pro-active attitude, you will see your results soar.

PART I

The Modern Evolution of Selling and Buying

1

The State of Sales Today

Sales professionals have always been masters at creating relation-ships where there were none to begin with. That hasn't changed, but now, we need to become masters at building twenty-first century relationships. It's no longer enough to put on a clean suit, practice the elevator pitch, and knock on doors. We can't just make cold calls to start sales conversations. Today, we need to extend our networks through technology and novel tools, then help our sales prospects interpret the abundance of information available to them online. Woody Allen was famously quoted as saying that "eighty percent of success is showing up." But showing up isn't enough anymore, because these days, you need to know exactly what you're doing when you get there.

> **Unfortunately, we rarely see the big, important trends in our lives as big and important while they're still working themselves out.**

So where do we start? How can we analyze the evolution in sales when we're right in the middle of it? Unfortunately, we rarely see the big, important trends in our lives as big and important while they're still working themselves out. We're too close. The changes keep happening in the background, and then one day, we wake up and realize that the world is different.

For example, the ubiquitous nature of the printed word seems like a given. Right now, I'm typing on my laptop in a coffeehouse, and as I look around, it seems that everyone is reading a newspaper, a magazine, their phone, or their tablet. But it's important to remember that the world wasn't always filled with printed material. For much of history, reading was the province of a select percentage of the population. It took hundreds of years for widespread literacy to become a thing. The world didn't change overnight when Johannes Gutenberg brought movable type to Europe and produced his first book in 1452. There was a gap between the invention and its widespread effect. By the time Columbus was sailing for the Americas forty years later, there were still only an estimated eight million printed books worldwide.

Those intervening decades must have been a tumultuous time for those making the books and those doing the reading. They were filled with questions like "What should we print?" or "Is reading an important skill?" And most importantly, "Who will even buy these books?" The printing press was a revolutionary technology, but even by 1800, only 12% of the world's population was literate. Literacy didn't take off until the twentieth century—in 1900, worldwide literacy was at 21%, and by 2000 it was 82%. So for something that seems so natural and normal, widespread literacy is actually a pretty new occurrence.[3]

The current technological revolution is happening much faster. It's not being measured in centuries, but in decades. According to Facebook, in December 2016 they had, on average, 1.15 billion mobile users every day.[4] That's over a billion people using a device that barely existed twenty years ago (not counting the bulky car phones that came with those over-the-shoulder carrying cases) to check into a social media site that was invented in 2004!

Amid these technological changes are larger societal changes that likewise impact sales strategies. Political organization, social organization, and business organization are all in flux, and as a result, sales practices that have been around for a generation or two are no longer working, and new ideas and techniques are popping up all over the place. It would be easier for us if we could name and catalog these changes in hindsight. But if we wait for hindsight, it would be too late for us to do anything about it.

Something we know for sure is that salespeople must continuously learn to incorporate new technologies and platforms into their interactions. For example, sales reps in many industries must develop and share a personal brand using social media platforms. E-newsletters, social media, video conferencing, blogs, and so much more have come into the picture. New artificial intelligence and CRM tools allow us to collect and parse through information, and there is always new data on the best times, days, and ways to reach out to prospects.

Meanwhile, some of the older techniques are no longer as effective. Calling prospects with the offer of some new tidbit or data point doesn't have the same appeal it did even ten years ago, because the new tidbit or data point is now just a Google search away. In order to thrive in this new environment, salespeople must offer their prospects something that Google can't.

The good news is that salespeople still have value to offer—services that can't be replicated by big data or the glut of online information. The complexity of this new sales world might be daunting at first, but it's actually a good thing for the profession. After all, if all aspects of selling were simple, they would all be outsourced to technology. In order to understand the unique value of the salesperson's role in the Hyper-Connected world, a good place to start will be to define what we mean when we talk about *sales*.

Creating the Sale in a Hyper-Connected Environment

It's not as easy to define "sales" as you might think. In many ways, "sales" and "selling" are words like "freedom" or "love." We all have a very good picture in our minds of what it means, but it only takes a short conversation to realize that our definition isn't universal. In fact, if you asked ten sales professionals to define "selling," you'd get ten different definitions in response. Or maybe eleven, because someone would change their mind after they heard what everybody else was saying.

The question is complicated further because there are a lot of salespeople out there. Depending on how you define selling, you come up with different numbers, but they're all pretty big. According to *Selling Power* magazine, in 2015 there were almost 2 million full-time salespeople in the United States, and about 24 million working in some capacity with a direct sales company.[5] If we assume that all of these people are going to approach selling the same way, we over-simplify the question. There's a wide range of activities that could be considered sales activities, so it follows that there has to be a broad scope for what sales is.

When you create an image in your mind of a stereotypical salesperson, what is it? Are you picturing a used car salesman in a bad suit trying to get you into a '97 Pontiac? Do you see a young kid at your local big box store in a polo shirt and nametag trying to sell you a refrigerator? Or do you see someone more professional, maybe a well-dressed woman selling a complex software package to the executives in a large corporation? These are all correct images—they're all salespeople. And so is the inbound salesperson sitting in a cubicle taking calls, the real estate or insurance salesman, the pharma sales rep visiting doctors, and the telemarketer calling during dinner.

> When you create an image in your mind of a stereotypical salesperson, what is it?

I recently did a search on LinkedIn and came up with 517,000 sales executives and 599,000 sales representatives.[6] But just because they have the same title doesn't mean these people do the same thing when they wake up in the morning. Assuming that all salespeople are going to approach their roles and their responsibilities the same way won't help us find the commonalities—and they do exist—between these jobs.

The salesperson at a retail mall store and the rep who sells multi-million dollar equipment packages don't have a lot of similarities on the surface. We need to go deeper to see the common threads that go through every sales career. And there is indeed one responsibility that every sales job requires. Without this key piece, the job might be marketing or consulting or business development, but it's not sales. When you dig down, at its core, every sales role is about one thing:

Creating the sale.

Notice I didn't say *getting* the sale, or *closing* to sale, or *finding* the sale. I choose these words carefully. Salespeople are creators. They create action. They create movement. Whether big or small, they make something happen. While the different steps required to make the sale happen aren't going to

> **Salespeople are creators. They create action. They create movement. Whether big or small, they make something happen.**

play out the same way for all sales professionals, the creation of the sale is fundamental for everyone. A mortgage broker is going to close a sale differently than an enterprise software sales executive, but at its heart, a sales job is about generating something that wasn't there before. A product or service comes into existence or has a purpose because of a salesperson's efforts. In fact, everything else—prospecting and getting leads, outreach, building relationships—is all in service of creating the sale.

There's an old sales adage that "Until a sale takes place, nothing happens." The saying is designed to make salespeople feel good about what they do, but it's also flat-out true. The act of selling is what moves business and life forward. Person A has a product or service, and needs to find someone who will pay them money to provide it. Person B has a problem they need solved or a gap filled, and is looking for a solution that they can buy. And the bridge between these two? The salesperson. It wouldn't make sense to run a widget factory if you couldn't sell any widgets, would it? It is always the salesperson who connects these two pieces of the puzzle.

Here are examples of how *creating the sale* is fundamental to so many different industries:

- It doesn't make sense to make artisanal cheeses if you can't sell them at a farmer's market.
- Everyone working at the auto factory can only get paid if the salesperson on the lot sells the car.
- You might be a great accountant, but until a partner brings in the client, you don't have any work to do.
- The programmers and engineers at a multinational technology company can't work on designing the web infrastructure for a national retail chain until the salespeople get a signed contract.

Selling Power magazine's study of the top 500 sales organizations shows that on average, each salesperson in the service or manufacturing industry supports 13.71 other jobs within the company.[7] That's amazing. All those other people wouldn't have their jobs if the sales rep wasn't out creating business. A host of activities are either started because of the sale, or justified because of the sale.

> The shift that's happening in the sales world is not in the "why" of sales, but in the "how."

All of this is still true in the Hyper-Connected world. The function of creating sales, of *making something happen*, hasn't changed. Successful salespeople will continue to stay true to that focus. In fact, it's more important than ever. The shift that's happening in the sales world is not in the "why" of sales, but in the "how." Sales professionals need to respond to the changes occurring in the different parts of their business lives. In fact, if they didn't respond at all, it would become almost comical.

My father had a short stint as an encyclopedia salesman before I was born. He went door-to-door and tried to convince people to buy the collected knowledge of the world in a beautiful leather-bound set of books that would impress your guests and help your children with their schoolwork. I remember his sample set sitting on our bookshelf when we were growing up, and they were gorgeous.

But would it make sense to sell encyclopedias door-to-door these days? Probably not, because not only has Encyclopedia Britannica shed its outside sales team, it has shed its books! Most kids probably think of going to Wikipedia before going to the bookshelf. And these changes are felt and seen well beyond the encyclopedia business. The internet has changed our level of access to information, and as a result, many of the industries and fields of yesterday have morphed into something new. So it's not just the way we buy and sell things that are changing; the products and services themselves are evolving faster than ever.

Technology-driven innovation means that the delivery and sales process has to keep up or fall into obsolescence. As we have seen, the core role of the salesperson—creating the sale—has nevertheless not changed. Taking this a step further, let's examine the new ways that salespeople create *value* during the sales process in today's Hyper-Connected landscape.

> **What our potential customers want and need has changed quite a bit, and we in the sales profession have to catch up.**

Providing Value, Then & Now

In today's selling environment, salespeople still must create the sale, but the specific strategies for doing this are changing. These strategies are dictated by what customers now consider to be *valuable* services during the sales process. What our potential customers want and need has changed quite a bit, and we in the sales profession have to catch up.

Value is another word, like sales, that has a different meaning for every person involved in the sales game. If we look at the sales process as inherently creative, *value* is what has been created during the sales process itself. It's what lies beyond the simple transaction. It's what's been added to the mix. It's the "sum is greater than the parts" element of sales.

In the past, adding value was as simple as letting customers know about the existence of a new product or service that could solve a problem. If you were a farmer in the late nineteenth century, when someone knocked on your door to show you a revolutionary plow that would save time and energy, this was a role that created value. In this case, the value point was making the customer aware of the product and what it could do. A little nearer to us, today's sophisticated B2B sales reps analyze their prospects' business processes to pinpoint possible new efficiencies within their software or distribution networks. These types of gains for the potential customer—whether they're measured in time, energy, attention, efficiency, cost, or peace of mind—are where the value in the sales process comes from.

In order to create value, we need to constantly be evaluating our prospect's and customer's needs. The top salespeople these days aren't the ones who are simply regurgitating information. Rather, they're finding new ways to address the gaps that their customers are trying to fill. For a salesperson to still have relevance in today's economy, they have to continue to be a bridge between the prospect who needs something and the company that has something. It's as simple as that.

Today's consumers are only a click away from online shopping carts, marketing automation, and robo-responders. This doesn't mean that salespeople no longer have a role to fill, but it *does* mean that the role has changed.

PayPal co-founder Peter Thiel mapped out where sales professionals can and can't compete with technology in his sermon to entrepreneurship, the book *Zero to One*.[8] In the middle of the book, he included a short section about how budding entrepreneurs market, sell, and distribute their new ideas. He argues that entrepreneurial products/services tend to fail not because of a bad idea, but because of inappropriate sales channels. He then lays out a spectrum of transactional amounts, from $1 all the way out to $10 million and above, breaking down three types of sales situations corresponding to these amounts.

It's not important to get hung up on the dollars and cents here—the analysis is geared to entrepreneurs, not salespeople. What's important is that these three sales situations show where sales reps can still provide value…and where they can't. Thiel's rule-of-thumb dictates that anything that can be automated will be, and anything that has some level of complexity will require a salesperson.

The first segment is what he categorizes as consumer-based purchases. For Thiel, these are products under $100, and it's what people are referring to when they say that sales is dead. It's a world filled with transactional sales. This is where sales automation is exploding, and these types of transactions are prevalent in some areas of the B2B world as well. These are the interactions that are being replaced with online buying. Customers are going to buy online if the sales transaction involves:

1. A relatively small dollar amount
2. Simple products or services (often a commodity)
3. Little need for explanation
4. Small amounts of risk from a bad purchase

These are scenarios where a salesperson can provide only a negligible amount of value. Because of that, it's more effective and efficient for people to buy from a website or catalog. Case in point: the rise of Amazon. As long as I know that the predictability of what I'm getting, along with the price, are at a certain comfort threshold, I'm totally fine with buying online. Even larger purchases like a big screen TV or similar appliances might be fair game.

For companies making these low-cost products, and the salespeople selling them, the world has changed dramatically. Consider the story of the Fuller Brush Company. In the middle of the twentieth century, the door-to-door Fuller Brush Man was such an iconic part of the culture that he made it into the movies (starring Red Skelton in the lead) and even into *Looney Tunes*.[9] Over 10 million families bought their household products from their local salesperson, and they became a trusted part of the community. You can see a great treatment of this in the 2002 movie *Door to Door*, with William H. Macy playing a local Fuller Brush salesman of over forty years.[10]

> For companies making these low-cost products, and the salespeople selling them, the world has changed dramatically.

But the world kept evolving, and as the movie showed, a lot changed in the life of a door-to-door salesman. These days, if you want to buy a Fuller product, you'll be waiting a long time for a knock on the door. You see, they don't even have a door-to-door sales force anymore. You can just go to their website: www.fuller.com.

Sales professionals can't much compete with the internet in these types of sales situations. Buyers like the convenience of online shopping. Advanced delivery systems mean that people can buy online and get their orders in just a few days, and in some places just a few hours. Deciding what to buy isn't that complicated, and reading online reviews and the like is enough to guide the buying decision. There's not much a sales rep can add to these commodity transactions, and because of that, the margins keep getting squeezed tighter. When pundits say that sales jobs are disappearing, these are the industries they're talking about.

It's on the other end of the sales spectrum, with its big price tags and long sales cycles, where salespeople still thrive. Thiel calls this the "big government and corporation" part of the spectrum, but we can think of this as the world of large consumer products (think houses) and B2B sales. On a completely practical level, the larger prices mean larger sales margins. On a functional level, more expensive products tend to be more complex, and where complexity exists, there is a need for someone to engage with potential buyers. These types of sales processes can't be left to marketing websites. Because there are many variables to consider and the risks of purchasing the wrong product are more acute, potential buyers want someone to help them through the process.

For example, think about the salespeople working with large tech companies like Dell or HP. They're selling hundreds, or even thousands, of computers to entire departments or buildings. The financial investment (and therefore the risk involved) is higher, the complexity is higher, and the need for skilled guidance is higher. In this scenario, the sales rep can't just walk in with an order form and ask how many the company needs. Rather, she will have to manage the process and ensure that the customer is getting a product that integrates well with the company's current equipment. It will also be important to ensure that the switch goes smoothly. Can you imagine how much money and productivity would be lost if an entire company didn't have computers for a week?

These scenarios have always needed a highly-trained sales force, but these days, the required skills are different.

> **Easy access to information means that salespeople now focus more than ever on relationship-building, problem-solving, and consultative selling.**

In the past, sales professionals were primarily providers of information. While they might not have admitted it, they were fancy brochure-deliverers or order-takers. As we'll examine further in following chapters, easy access to information means that salespeople now focus more than ever on relationship-building, problem-solving, and consultative selling. The sales professionals who can build trust with their prospects and then walk them through the long sales cycle will be the ones who survive.

In between these high-cost sales situations, where salespeople are still vital, and low-cost sales, where salespeople are disappearing, we find the middle bracket. This is the area of middling complexity and costs, such as car sales, insurance sales, and software-as-a-service (SaaS) offerings. These are areas where the sales evolution is most pronounced. It's still possible to be successful here, but salespeople have to adapt to the new world if they're going to succeed.

Peter Thiel describes this as the "dead zone" for entrepreneurs. According to Thiel, while these types of products and services don't lend themselves easily to online sales and marketing, they also don't always have the size, complexity, and profit margins to necessitate and support salespeople. Thiel warns entrepreneurs to steer clear of these industries, but it's not that simple. While these precautions might be relevant for entrepreneurs creating new businesses, there are many established industries with bountiful opportunities for sales professionals to be successful.

In this middle bracket we find a lot of "hybridization" of the sales process. Digital information and automated communication are becoming part of the process, but the human element continues to be important.

A perfect example of this hybridization is car sales. On the one hand, consider how substantially buying a car has changed because of the internet. We can pull up reviews, comparisons, and access a wide range of sellers right on our smartphones. If you're the buyer, you don't walk onto a car lot "blind." Instead, you're backed by a good deal of information that you'll use to inform your decision. At the dealership, though, you still work with people who hopefully use their experience and training to make sure you're making the best decision for your needs.

I bought a car recently myself, and I had the entire internet in my pocket on my smartphone. But it was the salesperson (also named David, so I liked him) who guided me and my wife to the car that we eventually bought.

Software-as-a-service (SaaS) offerings also provide a good example of sales hybridization. It has become common for software companies to offer freemium or low-cost options directly online, so it's possible to download a basic version and use it right away. The goal is to give a taste of the full capabilities and hook the potential buyer—these usually have a strong inbound marketing component as well. Once users have had a chance to test-drive the software, there's a concerted push to upsell them. This is where the salesperson enters the picture, and as they try to increase the size and scope of the initial purchase, the human element becomes more and more important.

In fields that are undergoing this hybridization, salespeople need to find if and where they can find a niche. In order to pinpoint the appropriate niche, salespeople must ask themselves whether they're providing *value* to their prospects. The first step is recognizing that these days, that value must go beyond simply providing information and taking the order. Salespeople must guide their prospects through the sales process in a way that's more meaningful, easier, or more efficient than what the customer can achieve on their own.

> **Salespeople must guide their prospects through the sales process in a way that's more meaningful, easier, or more efficient than what the customer can achieve on their own.**

As time goes on, sales positions in these "middle bracket" industries will increasingly resemble the sales and business development roles in the large, complex, "high bracket" sales cycles. Salespeople will need to guide and lead their prospects through the entire buying journey, rather than limiting their role to asking for business at the end of a single conversation. In short, salespeople will need to do what a website can't, and *this* is where the value in today's sales is centered.

The skills necessary for success in this environment aren't the same as the old-school ones. It's not just enough to have the resilience to make a lot of sales calls or handle rejection well. While those skills are still useful, the evolved sales professional will need to understand how to brand and market themselves as a resource for their prospects and customers. They need to focus on uncovering prospects' pain points and understanding their customers' needs. They need to help their prospects navigate the tremendous amount of information now easily available online, and they need to build trust so that the prospect returns when they're ready to make a purchase. Now more than ever, sales isn't about a single interaction, but rather about long-term relationships that create access, trust, and influence.

The sales profession isn't dying. We're not ready to buy everything and anything online. There is still a demand for experts to help people find and acquire the products and services they need. To be successful, though, sales professionals have to be willing to update their skillsets to mirror what their prospects actually need.

The world of the passive order-taker and the aggressive cold-caller has disappeared. Will you evolve or perish?

2

The 4 Stages of the Sales Evolution

In 1973, Arthur C. Clarke wrote a science-fiction novel called *Rendezvous with Rama*. It was a book about humanity's first encounter with an alien spaceship, and it won all sorts of awards. It was hailed as a visionary look at the near-future of science and civilization.[11] Clarke, who also wrote *2001: A Space Odyssey*, was a scientist and inventor who always referenced cutting-edge physics and technology in his books. *Rendezvous with Rama* was filled with all the up-to-the-minute science of the early '70s, and yet the protagonists didn't use computers to help them run their spaceship. They had, and I kid you not, trained monkeys. A technology that we can't imagine living without today wasn't even on the radar for a futurist a half century ago!

The computers and communicators of *Star Trek*, which first appeared around the same time *Rendezvous with Rama* was published, seemed much more fantastical and out-there. Gene Roddenberry was able to wildly imagine everyone having a personal device for communicating with others, but not until the far-future of the twenty-fifth century. It wasn't expected to happen any time soon.

Understanding the Pace of Technological Change

It's not a far stretch to say that technology has changed human life over the past few decades more than ever before in history. We live in a world of startling upheaval: digitization, globalization, urbanization…the list goes on and on. But we have difficulty seeing the totality of this change, because as humans, we tend to experience today as pretty similar to yesterday, which was pretty similar to the day before that. But if we go back ten or twenty years, the world really did look different, and going back one hundred years, the contrasts are stark. Think about how much has changed in the last one hundred years. Those few who are turning one hundred in the year 2017 were born the same year that the United States entered World War I! Over the course of their lifetimes they saw the mass adoption of cars, airplanes, televisions, and now, computers. Narrowing the time frame, think about the fact that MTV first took to the air in 1981, the same year that's pegged as the beginning of the "Millennial" generation. Since then, 137 million Americans have been born,[12] meaning that one-third of the American population doesn't know a world without MTV. (It's ironic that most of them don't even know that the M stands for music, which is what the station used to actually play.)

This is the generation that grew up alongside the personal computer. During the lifetime of a Millennial, computers moved from serving specialized business and academic functions to becoming central to people's lives. So these 137 million people came of age with computers as an expected part of their lives. This is why they're called "digital natives"—they don't know any other world. Especially for younger members of the Millennial generation, it's harder to notice the huge impact that technology has had, because for them, it's always been like this. And yet the change was actually quite recent: Windows came out in 1985, and the popular Apple IIe, which I used to write my first term papers, came out in 1983.

Humans are fundamentally wired to <u>not</u> see changes that are happening on large scales or over longer periods of time. Because of this, we end up making two mistakes when looking at our current situation. We tend to think, usually subconsciously, that:

1. The way the world is now is the way it's always been
2. It's going to stay the same and not change

We're great at building explanatory stories, but only when we're looking in the rearview mirror. In many ways, we can only see how things happen in hindsight.

> **Humans are fundamentally wired to <u>not</u> see changes that are happening on large scales or over longer periods of time.**

When personal computers were first introduced, they weren't seen as a tool that was about to revolutionize every aspect of our lives. Early computer manufacturers didn't know we would message each other with them, find maps with them, even control the thermostat in our house with them. Computers were marketed for spreadsheets and databases. One of the first personal computers was the Honeywell Kitchen Computer that came out in 1969 and cost $10,000 (almost $70,000 in today's money). It stored recipes.[13] But now that computers have come to touch every part of our lives, we create a story of inevitability about how they developed. Looking back in hindsight, we can identify all the signs and categorize the reasons for the computer's ascendance. Yet few of these signs were recognized during the '80s and early '90s when we were already neck-deep in an unprecedented technological revolution.

As salespeople, it's vital for us to recognize large-scale changes and trends while they're still happening, instead of in the rearview mirror. The most successful sales professionals are going to understand:

1. The way the world is now has changed dramatically from the past
2. It's going to keep changing

We don't have to know *exactly* where the road is going, but by being open to the changes that are happening, salespeople can take advantage of these changes instead of finding themselves in the obsolescence bin. If your approach to sales is, "We should do it this way because that's the way we've always done it," it's not a question of failing, but how fast you will fail. If you want to be successful in a Hyper-Connected world, you have to be willing to accept that things have and are changing, and the world that you learned how to sell in is different than the one we're in now.

The 4 Stages: Lacking Access, Awareness, Appreciation, Attention

In order to understand what sales is like today, it's important to first look at sales trends in the past. Jokes about sales being the world's oldest profession aside, the modern conception of the salesperson is only about 200 years old. Before that, there simply weren't enough products on the market to necessitate a separate group of sales professionals. There were plenty of merchants around, but they weren't salespeople like we think

> **Fundamentally, selling is about identifying and solving a need, a "lack" of something.**

of them today. They were just your local producers, and people would go to that particular merchant when they needed a horseshoe or salt or whatever else you couldn't make at home. Product differentiation and branding didn't happen in a meaningful way back then. Nobody had to "sell" in the way that we think about it.

But all that changed with the Industrial Revolution, the large-scale economic transformation that originated in Britain and eventually spread all over the world. As a result of the Industrial Revolution, many individuals, families, and local merchants stopped making their own goods in their own homes or villages. Products were now being mass-produced, often in faraway cities. Now there was a reason for sales activities to coalesce around specific professionals, and for salespeople to travel far and wide to distribute their products.

Fundamentally, selling is about identifying and solving a need, a "lack" of something. Selling is about creating a bridge between a prospect's need and the ability to fulfill that need. But the needs of sales prospects have changed over time, and in lockstep with that, the role of the salesperson has shifted. The salesperson's role has gone through four distinct phases over the last century and a half. The dates aren't exact, but the eras are easy to see:

Customers Lack Access: 1865-1920

In the second half of the nineteenth century, sales was all about introducing the products of a newly-industrialized economy to consumers. Before the Industrial Revolution took hold, there was no need for "selling" in its current conception because the demand for goods outpaced what could be supplied. Advancements in manufacturing and technology created a spike in our ability to create a supply that could meet, and then surpass, consumer demand. Improvements in everything from agriculture to transportation networks to assembly lines made it possible to make more stuff, faster. You could make everything from nails and cars to clothes and furniture at scale.

The birth of selling came about because of this explosion of productive capacity. Instead of just creating necessities, it was now possible to create everything faster and cheaper. Take something like clothing. When Levi Strauss got the patent to make pants out of denim (he used to make tents) in 1873, mass-produced clothing was a relatively new concept. This is something we take for granted, but for most of history, people didn't actually own that much clothing. You probably have more than one pair of blue jeans in your closet. In fact, you might have five or ten pairs. Before factories enabled the ability to scale production, that was unheard of. You had to make every piece of clothing by hand, which was time-consuming and expensive.

All of a sudden, it became important to find an outlet for this productive capacity. You had to get those blue jeans to the consumers, some of whom didn't know what blue jeans were, or didn't know where to find them.

Another example of the salesperson's newfound role is the popularization of selling aluminum products throughout the 1900s. Once upon a time, aluminum was so hard to produce that it was worth more than gold. It was considered such a splendid luxury that they made the original capstone of the Washington Monument out of aluminum in 1884.[14] Soon after, though, new production techniques made aluminum cheap to manufacture. Problem was, potential customers didn't know about these new products, and it became necessary for aluminum-producing companies to employ a legion of sales reps to go out and introduce them to the market. In the early 1900s, sales professionals connected the public with products ranging from aluminum foil to aluminum electrical wiring.

How else were you going to let people know about these life-changing products and services? Many sales people during this era worked in the new retail establishments that were springing up, including the new department stores in large cities. Many others were the traveling salesmen (almost all of them were men at this time) knocking on urban doors or crisscrossing the farms of the booming west. The most important focus for a sales rep during this time was getting their product in front of as many people as possible. Technological improvements were leap-frogging each other as invention and innovation were the words of the day, and salespeople needed to let prospects know about all the amazing new products that were out there.

Customers Lack Awareness: 1920-1960

By the end of the first World War, the industrial model was firmly entrenched. The wow factor of access to new products started to fade. It was no longer enough to simply put out a catalog or send a sales representative with a sample to someone's door. Like any market with a lot of opportunity, profits had attracted competition. It became important to do more than just show people your new shiny product, because now they had other options. The vacuum that had created the first gold rush, so to speak, was over. Add in the boom and bust cycles of the Great Depression and the war economies, and the focus of selling had deeply changed.

Potential customers now knew about all of the products and services that were available to them. They even knew how to get their hands on something they wanted. Companies now had to compete with each other for a slice of the pie, and multiple companies produced similar products. Salespeople needed to focus more on building awareness about their products and services, and how their product was superior to a similar product from another company. Modern marketing, advertising, and selling began to coalesce around this time.

Anything that revolved around getting the word out was important. Art moved from being a cultured pursuit to the province of graphic artists designing posters, newspaper advertisements, and packaging. Writers went from just writing novels to writing ad copy. F. Scott Fitzgerald was in advertising before he published *This Side of Paradise*. If you were good at talking, you went from politics and preaching into sales.

Instead of just letting prospective buyers know about what they were offering, salespeople had to show how their offerings were better than the rest. This is when the idea of brand names and brands in general took on increasing importance. It had always been important to share your quality, but now it was important to share your quality vis-à-vis your competitors.

Customers Lack Appreciation: 1960-2000

I don't use appreciation here in the sense of gratitude, but rather in terms of informed understanding. With the post-World War II economic boom, there were more products and services available than ever before, and a relatively prosperous society had more money for them. But the differences between options were smaller than they had ever been. The move from a horse-drawn wagon to a Ford pickup is huge, but the shift from a 1962 Chrysler to a 1963 Chrysler isn't nearly as nearly noticeable. It became increasingly important to differentiate your products and services from everyone else's, but at the same time those differences were smaller than ever.

Meanwhile, information became more prevalent because of technology. The rapid adoption of radio and television now meant that newspapers weren't the primary way to connect buyers with products and services. Phones became a much more common sight in homes and offices, as it actually wasn't until after World War II that more than half of American homes had them. All of these tools gave companies and their salespeople a host of avenues to use.

They needed every tool they could find, because they had to teach their prospects to appreciate the differences that set their offerings apart. Salespeople provided the latest information to help their clients make the best decisions. Instead of just telling consumers that the products were available, salespeople had to be the point of contact between their company and the end buyer, which often involved providing up-to-date information or research about product comparisons.

This time period makes me think of the phone approach I learned from the sales trainer Brian Tracy. I used to listen to his audio books on the cassette deck in my car. Tracy's technique went something like, "Hi Mr. Prospect, if I could show you how we could save you 15% on your productions costs, would it be worth 20 minutes of your time?" Inherent to this approach was the idea that the prospect lacks some critical piece of information. It assumes that the salesperson knows more than the prospect, and that the prospect should be glad to give up their time so they can stop using an inferior, old-fashioned product that is costing them time and money.

In this paradigm, the salesperson's job was to get in front of the prospect, then get them the information they needed in order to make a purchase. Salespeople had the information and the prospects didn't, so they could exert leverage over their customers and control the conversation. This information asymmetry was about to radically change.

Customers Lack Attention: 2000-present

The rise of the Internet in the last decade of the twentieth century heralded the most recent shift in the sales paradigm. Whether you call the new world a knowledge economy, a digital economy, or an information economy, it's clear that the computer, and the internet, fundamentally altered how we interact with each other. In doing so, it also destroyed the chokehold that salespeople held on information.

Prospects and customers can now find product details, including features and prices, with only a few clicks on a website. The journey to finding a better service provider or product often begins with a simple Google search. Now there are fewer surprises that a salesperson can offer their prospects.

No longer do prospects lack information. They have it in droves. But this glut of information comes at a price. Prospects now have overwhelming demands on their time and attention. Unfortunately, finding the right product is rarely as simple as typing in your needs and having the "Interwebulator 2000" spit out an answer. When a Google search can churn out millions of hits, it is hard to sift through everything. Buying something as simple as an airline ticket online can still cause confusion and stress because of the number of options available.

> No longer do prospects lack information. They have it in droves. But this glut of information comes at a price.

And time to digest all of this information is at a premium as well. In 2014, the average full-time worker in the U.S. logged 47 hours of work per week, with almost half logging over 40 hours.[15]

People are just flat-out busy. Adding to this overall noise and stress is definitely not going to win points with a prospect. Interrupting a prospect's day to provide more information has ceased to become a reliable way to get in front of customers

Instead, salespeople must now be advisors for their prospects, helping them navigate the increasingly complex buying process. Effectiveness has become much more about being a consultative problem-solver. Salespeople must now be not only experts in their fields, but experts at helping prospects make good decisions.

Looking to the Future of Sales

As we have seen, the sales profession isn't a monolithic entity that has been the same for centuries. The profession constantly changes and evolves as the needs of the economy have developed. Technology has created new opportunities and destroyed old markets. It would be funny to think of someone going door-to-door to sell anvils right now. It's easy to see the ridiculousness of that because of the time difference involved.

But what about the idea of cold-calling a house during dinner time and trying to get the family to change long-distance phone providers? That might not seem quite as ridiculous as selling anvils, but it's becoming about as effective. I remember those calls coming in during dinner when I was growing up, which wasn't that long ago, but in many ways it's a lifetime ago.

Salespeople now have to focus on building trust with long-term sales prospects. Today's sales professionals need to be relationship experts. Only then will they have the access and leverage to help move their prospects and customers along the buying journey. In the next chapter, we'll see how the internet has completely changed how salespeople should be approaching their prospects, because they aren't nearly as clueless as they used to be.

3

Is the End of Information Asymmetry the End of Sales?

R ecently I was at a cell phone store with my wife. She was in need of a new smart phone because she had dropped her old phone, causing a crack that went the length of the screen. She had lived with the crack for a few weeks, but it was definitely time to get a replacement.

After picking out a phone, my wife looked through the screen protectors hanging on a rack by the counter. The salesperson she was working with recommended a top-of-the-line protector, which was $29. It seemed like a small price to pay to protect her phone and prevent her from having to buy a new one again. Unfortunately for the salesperson, I was doing a little research on my completely functional device at the same time. It took only a minute to find a 4-pack online for $5.99 (with free shipping). A few clicks and we had saved ourselves 80% off the store's price.

This was just a small purchase, but the experience shows how easy access to information has changed the customer/salesperson dynamic. In the pre-internet world, information was at a premium, so sales reps could approach their prospect from a position of authority, and let's be honest, power. They knew more than their prospect about what they were selling, and they could use that power to steer the conversation in the direction they wanted. This made for some mistrust and suspicion on the customer's side, but for the salesperson, there were a lot of benefits to this information asymmetry. They could usually demand higher prices and shorter sales cycles because the customer couldn't easily shop around.

Then the internet came along and swept the legs out from under the sales profession. The World Wide Web connected people to information in a way that was simpler, easier, and much more efficient than ever before possible, and it quickly redrew the rules of engagement in the sales world.

Equality of Information Means More Trust

I first came across the term *information asymmetry* in Daniel H. Pink's *To Sell is Human*.[16] The term describes the imbalance in information between the salesperson and the sales prospect. Before the internet, rarely did both sides of this interaction have the same information at their disposal. It was the sales rep who had the high ground. The arrival of the internet evened the playing field, and truth be told, tilted it in favor of the customer.

If you're like me and have younger siblings, you might have tried to exchange nickels for dimes with them when you were a kid. You knew that the nickels were physically bigger, but only worth half as much. Your kid sister didn't know that, and so she took the trade thinking you were helping her out, because obviously bigger ones are better. If you were the younger sibling, you probably started trusting your big brother a little less when your parents found out and made him give the dimes back. That's information asymmetry in action. (By the way, sorry about that, Anna.)

For our purposes, it's not just about the different amounts of information on each side. It's about the effect of that imbalance when one side is trying to make a decision. In the situation with my sister, one person knew more than the other about what was being exchanged, and that had an impact on the exchange itself and who it benefited. Up until the advent of the internet, there was a lot of this information asymmetry in the relationship between prospects and sales professionals. While this gave the salespeople a great deal of power, it also led to strained trust. The prospect didn't know if they were getting a straight answer and a good deal. Most of the negative stereotypes about sales professionals stem from this imbalance.

> **Up until the advent of the internet, there was a lot of this information asymmetry in the relationship between prospects and sales professionals. While this gave the salespeople a great deal of power, it also led to strained trust.**

Think about the last time you went to the mechanic. The level of complexity involved with your car means that you can't find a YouTube video that lets you diagnose and fix the problem yourself. You need to go to an expert who has more information and knowledge than you do. You will have to buy parts and services you don't understand at prices you don't have a frame of reference for. If you don't know how an internal combustion engine works, you can't know for sure if the mechanic is making something up or if you really do need to rebuild the transmission.

There was a time not so long ago when every sales interaction was a little like this. You can imagine how this caused a general sense of uneasiness surrounding salespeople. For better or worse, things are different now. On-demand information is the norm, and while this has taken some power away from sales representatives, there's a big perk. It means the relationship between the salesperson and the prospect can now be built on trust.

The disappearance of information asymmetry in sales started with chat rooms and bulletin boards. Later, it developed into ratings websites, information portals, and of course, social media.

Today, any customer with easy access to the internet can get information from:

- Social media platforms
- Industry and association forums
- White papers
- Review sites like Yelp or Travel Advisor
- Blogs by influential industry experts
- Whatever pops up on a Google Search
- YouTube or other online video sites
- Company websites

This abundance of sources has created a new equality in information. The rules of engagement between salespeople and prospects have been re-written. In *To Sell is Human*, Pink writes, "...As the information advantage [that salespeople used to have] has withered, so has the power it once conferred. As a result, the ability to move people now depends on power's inverse: understanding another person's perspective, getting inside his head, and seeing the world through his eyes."

> The rules of engagement between salespeople and prospects have been re-written.

You can't just bulldoze or talk rings around a prospect anymore, because they'll get the information they need to make their decision whether you want to help them or not. This level playing field means that authority and power now have radically different meanings in the sales context. No longer can a used car salesman use a silver tongue and empty promises to sell a customer a lemon, because the customer can research VINs and purchasing histories in real time.

Look at what happened to life insurance premiums in the late 1990s. In a study published in 2000, economists Jeffrey Brown and Austan Goolsbee demonstrated that online comparison sites had a dramatic impact on the price of term-life insurance—to the tune of reducing the prices by between 8 and 15%.[17] Before the internet, life insurance prices were hidden behind a lot of charts and graphs, and it was almost impossible to do any sort of comparison shopping. The internet changed that, because now customers can actively find information on policies and compare rates. This caused the price to drop because companies (and salespeople) couldn't depend on prospects' ignorance.

Long term, this shift will do a lot to improve the relationship between prospects and sales professionals because it will rebuild trust. In the short term, though, the shift in information asymmetry is creating an identity crisis for salespeople.

Leading Prospects Through the Information Jungle

Back when sales professionals had the missing information their prospects needed, it was easy to see themselves as evangelists. They felt important. They alone could spread the word about their amazing product. In my knife-selling days, I remember a top rep telling me, "Everyone wants a set of our knives in their kitchen. They just don't know it yet. It's our job to show them what they were missing." When we saw ourselves as providers of important, hard-to-find information, we had a clear reason to engage with a prospect. It was good motivation to dial for dollars, push past the gatekeepers, and handle any initial rejection, because you could imagine that the prospect just didn't know what they were missing out on.

In this context, reaching out to prospects made sense. It wasn't an interruption of their day, but rather a chance for them to find out about a solution they didn't know they needed. For example, in the past, real estate agents had access to a book with all of the houses listed for sale in the area. If you wanted to buy a house, you had to engage with an agent to get access to that information. These days, of course, you can jump online and easily find the MLS (multiple listing service) entries for every property in the area. No real estate agent needed. Most properties even have URLs listed on their for-sale signs so you can check them out on your smartphone.

Many salespeople are left adrift in this new world. They were once information merchants, but there's no money in that anymore. Information is a now an accessible commodity, and people aren't going to answer a phone call to talk to a stranger promising a nugget of information.

The death of information asymmetry, though, doesn't mean that sales has faded into the past. Having more information, it turns out, doesn't necessarily make it easier to make decisions. Nor does it lead to better decisions.

A growing body of research is showing that humans aren't as adept at processing information as we think we are. Columbia researcher and author of *The Art of Choosing*, Sheena Iyengar, found in a 2004 study that the opt-in rate for a company's 401(k) plan actually fell as more and more options were given. Fewer people joined the program, and the ones who did join picked options with a lower return.[18] In another experiment run by Eric Kessler at Pace University's Lubin School of Business, two groups of MBAs were asked to pick stocks for a make-believe portfolio. One group was bombarded with information from stock analysts and experts. The other group was just shown the prices as they changed. The group that only saw the prices ended up with double the return than the information-soaked group.[19]

> Information is now an accessible commodity, and people aren't going to answer a phone call to talk to a stranger promising a nugget of information.

People are bad at making decisions when they are overwhelmed with information. In his bestselling book *Blink,* journalist Malcolm Gladwell popularized another experiment done by Sheena Iyengar.[20] She set up a display in a fancy grocery store, then offered one group of shoppers 24 types of jam, and another group only six. When offered six choices, almost 30% of potential customers bought jam.

When they had 24 options, only 3% bought jam. They were overwhelmed by the options.

Humans, it turns out, aren't physically wired to handle too much information. In an experiment at Temple University, researchers put people into fMRI machines and watched as they made decisions for combinatorial auctions, a massively complex type of bidding strategy that requires a lot of brain bandwidth.[21] By looking at the brain while it was working, researchers found that the higher-functioning parts of the brain would essentially become exhausted by the process and shut down. At that point people would start making impulsive decisions driven by emotion. In other words, the idea of information-overload isn't a metaphor. It actually happens in the brain.

So while there is more and more information available to sales prospects, in some cases this might actually be causing them to make poor choices, or get stuck and make no decision at all. This is where sales professionals can help. Today, it's not about bringing information to the prospect. It's about being translators, interpreters, and guides.

As we will soon see, this new role is the key to finding success in the Hyper-Connected world. But this isn't necessarily an intuitive evolution for salespeople who are accustomed to being proactive, assertive change-makers, because the best way to succeed today as a sales guide is to take a back seat and let someone else drive. It's time to give up the control and let our prospects show us what they want.

By looking at the evolving sales world through the perspective of our prospects, the next steps forward become pretty obvious. Buyers are on their own journeys. Let's tag along and let them show us where to go.

4

The Buyer's Journey in the Twenty-First Century

There's a statistic out there that gets thrown around so often by advocates of social selling that it's become a bona fide meme. The number is supposed to prove that the world has changed, and salespeople need to adapt to stay relevant. It's a reference from a 2011 study by the CEB Sales Executive Council finding that typical customers have already completed 57% of their buying journey before even contacting a supplier.[22]

The implication is that more and more of the research is being done by prospects before a sales professional begins to influence the process. And if that's the case, it's also an indication that the old style of "interruption selling" isn't going to work like it used to.

Let's look at what this statistic could mean. If you're like me, you might be highly suspicious as to how much weight should be given to a single study. In this case, delving deeper into the situation reveals that more research has backed up the finding. In 2013, the Sales Benchmark Index found from their own studies that the percentage had actually jumped to 65%.[23] And a 2012 IT Buyer Experience study by IDC reported that an average of nearly 50% of the purchasing process for technology solutions was complete before a salesperson became involved.[24] Similarly, a 2015 Forrester Research survey showed that 74% of business buyers reported conducting more than half of their research online before making an offline purchase.[25]

Taken together, it's obvious that something has changed. Prospects are starting the buying process well before engaging with a salesperson, and this is a direct result of increased access to information. Now it's the customers who are in control of the sales process, because they arrive at the bargaining table with their own research and information.

> **Prospects are starting the buying process well before engaging with a salesperson, and this is a direct result of increased access to information.**

Buying a TV, Then & Now

Sales professionals already know what it's like to be on the other side of the table, because all of us are also buyers. Consider something as simple as buying a TV. Going back fifty years, we find a relatively straightforward process. Back then, when you decided you wanted a new TV, you'd go to your local appliance or electronics store. There might have even been a dedicated television store if you lived in a big enough city. You'd walk in having only limited knowledge about different brands based on advertisements that you saw. You'd find a salesperson working the floor and tell them you wanted to look at televisions.

And from that point forward, you were in the salesperson's hands. He would show you the choices, describe the differences, try to get you hooked on the most expensive one, and get your payment. That was that. Sure, you might have asked your friends about what TVs they liked beforehand, or maybe you wanted one like the Joneses' across the street, but it was a relatively closed loop. If you wanted to get more information or do some comparison shopping, it was cumbersome and challenging. It was usually easier to just buy whatever the salesperson convinced you to take home.

Compare this to the modern process of buying a television. Your first trip, once you decide that the living room needs a new TV, won't be to the store. It will be to your computer, or maybe your smartphone will suffice. You can surf review sites, look at the ratings for different televisions online, and compare prices on the websites of your local retailers. You can post a question on your favorite social media platform and ask your connections about their preferences and suggestions. After that, you might narrow down the search to a small handful of options, and from there, depending on your price point and how comfortable you are with your decision, you might buy it through Amazon or BestBuy.com.

But if you still have some questions, or if you want to see what it looks like in person, you'll take a trip to your local Best Buy or big box retailer. You are going in as a highly informed buyer. At this point in your journey, you aren't looking to begin the information-gathering process from scratch. Instead, you're looking for someone to help you translate what you already know into a usable form. You might not know the difference between HD or 4K HD or whether you should have a smart TV. The salesperson's job is to help take you through the final stages of your buying process.

Even if you hadn't had the chance to do as much research beforehand as you would have liked, information is available to you in real time on your smartphone, which you might very well use while you're in the store. The salesperson has to acknowledge and work with the fact that you aren't an empty vessel to fill up and push around. Whether you're looking for a TV, car, or house for your personal life, or a new CRM or expense report app at work, as a buyer you're an active participant in the buying process.

This is the buying journey that *your* Hyper-Connected prospects are going through right now. If you're trying to sell your customers like a 1960s TV salesperson would, you're in trouble. That's the road to obsolescence. Treating your prospects as if they don't know anything about the product would be highly counterproductive, and you risk alienating or even upsetting them.

Sales professionals don't have to fear the newly-empowered buyer, but we do have to engage with them differently. There are a lot of potential potholes and forks in the road in the buyer's journey, and our role is to help them navigate through it. Buyers don't want to let you drive, but they *do* want someone to help them navigate. This is where salespeople create the value that we spoke about earlier in the book.

If you're like many salespeople I know, you might be bristling at the thought of just helping a prospect across the finish line. I can hear you yelling: "I'm not selling TVs at Best Buy! I do way more than help people decide between the 55- and 60-inch screen!" You might point out that salespeople are critical to finding prospects and starting conversations. That we still need to build value, to close the sale, and all the other little bits in between.

And you're right! These aspects of the sales role are still important. The key is to remember that the new salesperson is contextual. It's his or her job to fit into the larger landscape that the prospect is engaging

> **The key is to remember that the new salesperson is contextual.**

with. This isn't the world of the lone gun-slinger anymore. This is an interconnected and highly-integrated world. There's power in realizing the sea that your prospects and customers are sailing in. Instead of fighting against the currents, learn how to work with the tides.

Let's take a look at how this new role plays out practically. When the product or service is more complex than buying a TV, there are a lot of places where a salesperson can build value.

Dan and Maria Buy a House

Buying a house is one of the most important purchases in the average homebuyer's life, but most of us aren't experts at the home-buying process. On average, Americans move less than twelve times in their lives, and you can assume that most of these moves don't involve an actual home purchase.[26] Homebuyers can't always fall back on experience when making their decisions. In the old days, they would call their local real estate agent, share which neighborhood they were interested in, and visit a bunch of houses with the agent. There would be a set list of preferred attributes, like the number of bedrooms or the quality of the kitchen. Buyers would lean heavily on the agent's knowledge and input on what constituted a good buy. It was a relatively simple process, and buyers depended on the salesperson for most of their information.

These days, though, it's a little different. Let's say Dan and Maria want to buy a house. They have two young children, they're making a little more money, and they want space to grow into. Before picking up the phone to call their real estate agent, though, they do their own research. They don't even leave their couch. They just pull out their cellphones on a Sunday afternoon and start hunting around. They start by looking up what they can sell their current condo for, using sites like Zillow.com. Then they go to sites that rate schools and look at the districts in the neighborhoods they're interested in. They look at the amenities, like parks and restaurants, in different neighborhoods. They do a Google maps search to see how long the commute would be to Maria's office. Then they look up the MLS (multiple listing service) online and get a complete list of the available homes in the areas they're interested in, along with how much they cost.

It wasn't until the early 2000s that the highly-coveted MLS was widely available online. Before that, the ability to research and list properties on a MLS was available only to real estate agents who subscribed to the service. They were the guardians of that information.

They were paid a premium by their clients because they held the keys to access. Back then, it was just as hard to sell your house on your own because, again, if someone couldn't get their house listed on the MLS, nobody would know it was available—and you can be sure that real estate agents weren't bending over backwards to help anyone who tried to cut them out of the process.

Now, by the time Dan and Maria have decided to engage with a real estate agent, they have a good idea of where they want to look, what's important to them, and what they can afford. There's a folder on their computer and a notebook on the desk in their home office chock full of notes, stats, graphs, and charts. They have looked at pictures online, and a number of postings included video tours as well.

These photos and online video tours have become pivotal to the home-buying process. Just over half of all homebuyers first saw the home that they eventually bought online.[27] But that doesn't mean they were ready to reach out and make an offer at that point. Customers might have houses in mind that look great based on online photos, but when they first contact an agent, their process is far from over. They need someone to help them make sense of the information they have compiled, to bring some experience to bear on the hidden risks and rewards, and to help them get the home they want at the price they want.

Who is that person going to be? Do they just call someone they see advertising on a local bus stop bench? Maybe. But what usually happens is more complex, and perfectly demonstrates how the Hyper-Connected salesperson gets involved in the buyer's process even before it starts.

The traditional thinking would be for a real estate agent to constantly ask people if they're looking to buy or sell a house. You'll get lucky eventually if you just keep asking, right? The Hyper-Connected salesperson takes a longer view of the process. A clever real estate agent knows that if they create and maintain long-term relationships, they'll have a huge advantage. Agents want to be the first person their contacts think of when it's time to buy or sell their home. These are long-term investments, but they tend to eventually pay off in a big way. Instead of trying to convince their prospects to move—a pestering strategy that doesn't work anyway—the patient agent makes themselves the obvious choice when the time comes. This is where the networking and branding that we will look at in the second half of the book comes into its own.

This is what happens in Dan and Maria's situation. A few years before they decided to move, Dan met John—who sells residential real estate for a local brokerage—while playing softball. Dan and John had a number of conversations over the years, but John was never pushy or obnoxious. He never once told Dan, "The rates are so good right now that you should really look to move." He never pressured Dan, but he *did* send out an e-newsletter every month, and he's active on Facebook and LinkedIn. What's more, John helped connect Dan and Maria with a mortgage broker who helped them refinance their current condo, and he invited the family to his holiday party, where he brought together clients, colleagues, and friends to mix and mingle. When Dan thought of real estate, he thought of John. It was an easy phone call to make.

Once Dan and Maria start to work with John, interpreting information becomes a big part of John's role. He facilitates the process. Dan and Maria don't know how to analyze all of the information in the MLS entry, but John knows what "cozy," "vintage," and "located by transportation" might really mean (small, old, and next to the highway). John has been selling in the area for a while, so he has information that is hard to uncover, like problems at one of the schools, or a new shopping development that's coming. John is also an expert at helping his clients decide what's really important to them. Beyond that, he can act as a quarterback and help his buyers assemble the entire team that is necessary when buying a home. He connects them with mortgage brokers, attorneys, appraisers, inspectors, and contractors.

Dan and Maria represent today's typical homebuyers, but of course there are outlying situations. There will still be some who don't have the time, attention, or inclination to do pre-research. In that scenario, an agent like John still fills the traditional role of information-provider. On the other side of the spectrum are prospects who walk into the first meeting with their decision all but made. All they'll need John to do is help with the price negotiation and paperwork. From John's perspective, it's important to know how to fill each of these roles, depending on the needs of the client.

So even with the explosion of information available to buyers, good real estate agents are as valuable and relevant as ever. In 2014, the Bureau of Labor estimated there were more than 400,000 active agents in the United States alone.[28] They aren't going anywhere. Dan and Maria had access to mountains of information and stacks

> So even with the explosion of information available to buyers, good real estate agents are as valuable and relevant as ever.

of data, but they didn't necessarily know what to do with it, and were grateful to have John help them through the process.

Buying in the B2B Context

On the surface, B2B sales doesn't seem as personal as selling a house to a family. In practice, though, B2B sales can be surprisingly intimate, and interpersonal skills are just as important. If you're selling enterprise-level software, heavy machinery, or HR services, you're selling directly to other people, and at its core, these people are approaching their buying journey with the same seriousness with which they make purchases in their personal life. The only difference is there tend to be even more variables in a business environment.

The additional layers of complexity start with the number of people involved in the decision. The Gartner Group found that in a typical firm with 100-500 employees, on average there are seven employees involved in most buying decisions.[29] Instead of just two domestic partners buying a home, in a B2B sale there might be everyone from decision-makers to end-users to internal and external champions. That's a whole lot of cooks in the kitchen. Meanwhile, the product might be many orders of magnitude greater in complexity. Sure, buying a house can be challenging, but how about buying an office building, a factory, or an entire company? Even a book-keeping software package for a medium-size company has layers of moving parts and different inputs and outputs. The business world is a noisy place.

Let's say that a sales department in a small organization is looking to bring in a new CRM system. I've seen this process unfold, and it's messy. There will probably be a sales manager (or three), a sales director, a VP of sales, an IT executive, an HR

> **Once the sales professional is brought in, they need to respect all of the activity that has already occurred.**

representative, and someone from finance all involved in the decision-making. This isn't new. There were always people from different departments and levels of the hierarchy involved. But now, in the Hyper-Connected world, each of these players does their own research and develops strong opinions and perspectives. The Director of Sales comes to one conclusion based on her research, while the VP of sales has gone down a completely different road. The first sales manager has been reading articles on a particular blog and is a big fan of a nimble cloud solution, while another is convinced that Salesforce is the way to go.

This is the "research before engaging with a salesperson" phase. Once the sales professional is brought in, they need to respect all of the activity that has already occurred. Every interaction they have with a prospect has to fit into a larger context. And the context is getting more and more complex.

A 2016 B2B Buyer's Survey from DemandGen found that more than half of respondents had seen an increase in the time it took to make a buying decision. Over 80% said this was driven by more research time, and over 70% said it was because more resources were being used to evaluate purchases. Additionally, over half the companies reported that there had been an increase in the number of people involved in buying decisions over the last year.[30] In this environment, it's critical for salespeople to keep their ears to the ground for what's happening in their prospects' worlds, and in the industry in general. A salesperson's biggest champion in an organization might not be the decision-maker, and the decision-maker might not be the end user.

It's easier than ever for new information to enter the stream at any time, and sales reps need to be responsive to the changing dynamics of the process. As Hank Barnes from the Gartner Group writes, "...buyers don't compartmentalize their decision process. Because of free access to information, they explore (consider buying), evaluate (consider alternative options), and engage (decide who to work with) at the same time."[31] So not only is the decision-making process incredibly complex, but buyers are bringing sales people into the process much later and expecting different levels of support.

> It's easier than ever for new information to enter the stream at any time, and sales reps need to be responsive to the changing dynamics of the process.

Buyers tend to get to a point where their internal research hits a wall. They have too much information, and not enough skill to decipher, analyze, and act upon it. When Hubspot released the results from their 2015 Sales Perception Survey, over 60% of prospects said they wanted to first engage with a salesperson when they hit this point of information overload. Only 19% wanted to talk to a salesperson when they were first starting the process.[32]

This moment—when a prospect hits that point of confusion and information overload—is a pivot point, and Hyper-Connected selling, in many ways, is about capitalizing on this. A B2B sales rep wants to be the person who prospects reach out to when they reach the pivot point. Sales reps need to be seen as micro-influencers in their specific field. They need to be the natural person to call.

In the study of behavioral economics, there's a phenomenon called the *availability heuristic.* A heuristic is just a mental shortcut used when making decisions, and the availability heuristic describes our tendency to over-value information that we've come across recently. That's why it's also called the *recency* heuristic. This is why salespeople need to stay in front of their prospects and clients as much as they can. They need to be the first person their networks think to reach out to.

Because the salesperson isn't necessarily in the room during a prospect's pre-research, they need to be constantly influencing the conversation in other ways. Remember John in the home-buying example? He connected with Dan and Maria well before they were actually prospects. He played softball with Dan, sent him monthly e-newsletters about real estate, and invited him to holiday parties. While networking in the B2B context might not be as personal as a holiday party, it's just as critical to stay connected. It's valuable to use things like social media channels, email marketing, and other platforms to provide information for prospects to digest and use during the initial phases of their research. Even a short conversation at a conference can position the salesperson in the mind of a prospect.

All of this work, of course, is directed toward eventually securing a sale. The goal is to be a salesperson, not an unpaid consultant. The prospect is looking to solve a specific problem, and sales reps want to position themselves as the person who will end the pain associated with that problem.

In the end, whether it's a new car for the family or a new technology platform for the company, the buyer's journey has gotten both easier and harder at the same time. Access to information has leveled the playing field between buyers and sellers, but this altered power dynamic hasn't removed the need for a salesperson. Rather, it's reframed their role. Salespeople are no longer glorified brochure-deliverers. Instead, the top sales professionals in the Hyper-Connected world are becoming guides and advisors. Let's now turn to exploring this exciting new role: that of the Sales Sherpa.

PART II

The Old School is the New School

5

From Gatecrasher to Guide: Becoming a Sales Sherpa™

"I know Kung Fu."

With those words from *The Matrix*, Keanu Reeves declared himself a true badass for a generation of black-leather-clad wannabees. (We'll ignore the questionable qualities of the other two movies in the trilogy for now.) *The Matrix* was released in 1999, the same year I became a sales manager. In fact, I snuck out of the office to see a matinee during its opening week.

Neo would use his Kung Fu throughout the rest of the movie, but it wasn't that line that stuck with me through my sales career. Instead it was a line delivered by Neo's mentor, Morpheus:

"I can only show you the door. You're the one that has to walk through it."

Maybe it was because I was young and impressionable. Maybe it was because I was just learning how to be a coach for my team. But that idea stuck with me and became a core principle of how I worked with my staff. It reminded me a lot of the old saying, "You can lead a horse to water, but you can't make it drink."

Back then, *The Matrix* provided the metaphoric yin to the yang of the sales culture I had been exposed to. Before my Morpheus-facilitated epiphany, I had felt that my job was to cajole, push, motivate, exhort, and do just about anything else to make my sales reps do more and sell more. That was the philosophy of sales and sales management I had been exposed to as a young professional in the '90s. The culture of the day relied on pushing. As a sales manager, you pushed sales reps to make calls, pushed prospects to see you, and then pushed them to sign on the dotted line. It wasn't always the most pleasant environment to work in, and it couldn't have been much fun for prospects and customers either. The general wisdom, though, was that selling was a battle, and you had to fight for success.

The Old-School Gatecrashers

There's another sales movie that came out when I was a young sales-person, and it stands as a pretty significant counter-example to the philosophy that *The Matrix* espoused. This movie was *Boiler Room*, and it seemed to glorify illegal gambling dens, drug-fueled excess, and hyper-aggressive dialing for dollars. In my opinion, coming out as it did in 2000, this film portrays the last hurrah of an old sales world that was disappearing with the old millennium.

If you haven't seen it (and you should), *Boiler Room* is the late 20th-century version of *Glengarry Glen Ross*. It follows the up and down career of Giovanni Ribisi's character, Seth Davis, who goes from running an illegal casino in his house to selling junk bonds over the phone. It's an interesting morality tale, but for many of my colleagues, the true fun was in the actual boiler room scenes.

When I first saw the movie, I was a sales manager recruiting college kids to sell Cutco knives. The job was a direct sales gig, as old-school as you could get. We were all young, we were all inexperienced, and our office culture definitely depended on exuberance and energy to make up for that. Even though we worked only by referral and weren't cold-calling like the characters in the movie, the portrayal of selling as a challenging competition that only the best could succeed at appealed to our egos.

There's a reason the sales culture was like it was. Facing rejection is one of the most challenging parts of a sales job, whether it's in recruiting, prospecting, or closing. One of the ways to handle this psychologically was to look at the situation as a battle. In this environment, more activity led to more success, and you had to figure out how to create as much activity as possible. If you heard "no" a lot, you had to develop psychological tricks to rile yourself up to stay in the game. We were dealing with rejection on a daily basis, and so we used the same tactics that salespeople had been using for decades to deal with it. In *Boiler Room*, just as in our daily lives, we were fighting against our colleagues, against our competitors, and even against our prospects. Of course, the movie is full of Hollywood hype and drama, but it connected to a very real thread in sales through the '70s, '80s, and '90s. The goal was to go to war, every day, for the customer's time, their business, and their money. Our customers were inside the fortress, and our job was to get past the walls and retrieve the spoils of war.

If this sounds a little extreme, think of the term we use to describe the people standing between a salesperson and their prospect: gatekeepers. These were the receptionists, assistants, and voicemail systems blocking access to the prospect. There were (and still are) books, seminars, audio programs, and articles with the sole focus of teaching you how to beat the gatekeeper. Because in the old paradigm of sales, you were the gatecrasher.

As a gatecrasher, your mission was unambiguous: to get past the gatekeeper. It might be human or electronic, but we had to get past them. If the prospect had a secretary, you could come up with clever ways to sweet-talk your way past them. If you were making cold calls, you could try early in the morning, or after five o'clock. If you wanted prospects to read a letter you sent, you could FedEx it so they'd think it was important. If it was a technological gatekeeper, there were hosts of voicemail tricks and tips to get your call returned. When email came on the scene, experts came up with tools and structures that would drive response rates, regardless of what you were selling or if the prospect needed it. Any obstacle between you and your goal had to be circumvented or defeated in any way possible.

You can see this culture of aggression in the exalted concept of the "hustle" in the sales world. The ability to work really hard and keep working was praised, because you were always being exhorted to go "into the breach" one more time. Within this sales paradigm, everyone was always talking about "attacking:" Attack your goals, attack the phone, and definitely attack your prospects' objections.

One of the most famous lines from *Glengarry Glen Ross,* the now-classic film about real estate salesmen, seems to have been added, by some unspoken law, to every sales book: "Always remember the ABCs of sales: Always Be Closing." Within this sales culture, you had to look at every interaction as a gladiatorial combat, with only the strong coming out alive. To use another movie line, this one from *Mad Max: Beyond Thunderdome:* "Two men enter. One man leaves!" In many ways, it didn't even matter if you were good at the actual process of selling. The idea was that if you worked hard enough, you'd be successful.

The ultra-competitiveness, the rejection, the sacrifice were all there on a daily basis. But if you bought into it, everything was made OK when you got the customer to say "yes." Your ego fed off the commission checks, the contest payouts, and the respect and adulation of your peers. Sure, it was hard and demanding, but there was a cultishness to it. The reigning philosophy was that only the best survive, so if someone wants to do it another way, that's because they couldn't hack it.

There's a saying in the military that generals are often stuck fighting the last war they fought in. Today, too many sales professionals are stuck waging battles like the guys in *Boiler Room*, and it just isn't working for them anymore. Clinging to this battle mentality has become both exhausting and fruitless. When you look at turnover rates in sales organizations, they can be quite telling. A Bridge Group survey in 2015 found that the average rep turnover rate (excluding promotions) in B2B SaaS companies was 34%. That number is over double the average turnover in non-sales positions.[33]

As one salesperson said to me in a hotel bar in Austin, Texas: "We're supposed to make call after call after call, and just play the numbers game. Well, our numbers are 2%. Two percent! That sucks. Why can't we figure out a better way of doing it? Because I'll tell you, this ain't fun."

This man's frustrations are borne out far beyond his personal experience. Salespeople feel incredibly disheartened when all of their activity bears little success. And with ever-changing advances in technology, it can feel like an arms race. With every new communications advance, whether it's predictive analytics, AI, or a fancy content curation platform, there seems to be another wall that shields prospects. And even without all of these high-tech gatekeepers, it's increasingly difficult to get in front of prospects simply because they don't have attention to spare. Who needs an email filter when you get hundreds of emails a day? It's easier to just ignore them. I once coached a Chief Marketing Officer for a large tech company on her social selling presence. Do you know how many unanswered invitations to connect she had in her LinkedIn account? Just north of 2,100, and that doesn't include the messages and Inmails that were waiting for her.

In the old days, if a salesperson couldn't convince their prospect to set up an appointment, that salesperson was a failure. They weren't going to make money, they might lose their job, and according to *Glengarry Glen Ross*, they were going to go thirsty, because coffee was for closers. But these days, the single-minded sprint for appointments isn't as important, and can even be detrimental. Our reputations precede us, and if we have a track record of treating people poorly and being pushy, it will catch up to us.

In today's Hyper-Connected environment, trying to be a gatecrasher is exhausting, not to mention ineffective. The good news is, there's another way of doing things.

> **In today's Hyper-Connected environment, trying to be a gatecrasher is exhausting, not to mention ineffective.**

Becoming a Sales Sherpa™

When salespeople look at their prospects as someone they have to "close," it's hard to see them as partners. This is a big problem, because seeing prospects as partners is exactly what's needed in today's sales landscape. Many sales reps who came up in the old culture are struggling to transform how they sell.

Even back then, the battlefield philosophy of sales was starting to wear on both the salespeople and the buyers. Years of looking at our prospects as opponents got tiresome. When you woke up every morning thinking that your job was to push past your customer's defensive walls, you felt worn down. It took a lot of energy and mental fortitude to keep doing this every day.

The battlefield mentality hasn't disappeared from sales, but it's losing its relevance. The Hyper-Connected world doesn't offer a lot of room for gatecrashers who are locked in permanent battle with their customers. There's too much transparency in the selling process now, and it's really not that effective.

Instead, as we saw earlier, the most effective sales professionals are acting as trusted advisors, helping the people they work with make better decisions. These top salespeople are what I call **Sales Sherpas**. These Sherpas lead their prospects through the overwhelm of information available, eventually helping them to the summit of a successful purchase.

If you've ever read about the challenges of climbing Mt. Everest, you know that a new climber is faced with a lot of unknown variables. The Sherpas are local people who have climbed the mountain before. They know the best paths, they know where the hidden obstacles are, like huge ravines and glaciers, and they know how to move past them. In fact, there's evidence that over the generations, Sherpas have become more adept at handling the lower oxygen and air pressure levels that accompany higher altitudes.[34] When climbers go to Mt. Everest, they have the end goal of summiting the mountain and standing on its peak. The Sherpa's job is to help them achieve that goal.

> The most effective sales professionals are acting as trusted advisors, helping the people they work with make better decisions.

Just as Sherpas use their local expertise to help novice climbers achieve their end goal, modern sales professionals need to integrate themselves into their prospect's buying journey in a way that is authentic, helpful, and effective. This is where we come back to Morpheus's quote about guiding Neo to the right door. Morpheus had an end goal. He knew what he wanted to do: He wanted to sell Neo on being "The One." But he didn't hammer Neo with value propositions and objection cycles. He worked alongside Neo as Neo worked through his own journey. Of course Morpheus was leading the process, but he wasn't forcing the situation to go exactly as he wanted. In many ways, they were walking side by side, with Morpheus just a little out front, pointing to important facts or decision-making points.

Your goal in the Hyper-Connected world is to become a trusted guide. As a Sales Sherpa, you guide prospects up the mountain of their buying journey as they confront the treacherous and confusing terrain of the modern marketplace. When things are tough, confusing, or challenging, the Sales Sherpa is there to help. They are the experts who have traveled the path up the mountain already. They can lend their perspective and knowledge to the people they work with.

This is a big switch from being a gatecrasher. Instead of viewing ourselves as an invading army trying to get past the gatekeeper, sales professionals now work to get inside the village before gates are ever needed. Instead of battling prospects, we can truly partner with them and help them move towards their goals. In the past, some top sales people did already possess this mentality, and a lot of others claimed that they did. Now, though, everyone needs to learn how to walk the walk.

It's tempting to dismiss the idea of being a Sales Sherpa as a Pollyanna fairy tale. For some, this all sounds too nice and easy. But just because it isn't defined by aggressiveness doesn't mean it's easy. Partnering with a prospect is much different than controlling them, and in many ways it's more difficult. We aren't trying to manipulate them through our process, but walk with them through theirs. When we give up that control, we open ourselves up to uncertainty and insecurity, but having the strength to work in this new paradigm is where the new power lies.

> When we give up that control, we open ourselves up to uncertainty and insecurity, but having the strength to work in this new paradigm is where the new power lays.

The Sales Sherpas have an incredibly challenging and complex role. They have to put in the time and effort required to develop true expertise. They have to build up a network of prospects and customers. They have to communicate and lead the people who have put their trust in them, and they have to be able to create that trust in the first place. Then they have to navigate the "mountain" and all of the spontaneous opportunities and challenges that present themselves during the journey.

It's a long-term play, but it's becoming the optimal play in the Hyper-Connected sales landscape. I know top salespeople who send referrals to their competitors if they aren't the right fit. Why would they do that? Because they have a long-term mindset. I have heard so many massively successful salespeople say, "If we're not the right solution, I'd rather have my prospect go with someone else. If they go with us and we're not right, they'll be unhappy, and we aren't going to get good business. That doesn't help anyone."

We humans aren't necessarily wired to have this long-term vision for our success. The sales professional who passes on business that's not right doesn't do it easily or lightly. She knows that she has to hit her sales goals and quotas. It would be simpler to just take everything that comes her way. It requires discipline and effort to invest in relationships now to get a return in the future, but there are also tangible payoffs that reward this focus.

> It requires discipline and effort to invest in relationships now to get a return in the future, but there are also tangible payoffs that reward this focus.

I know a wealth advisor who works with many high-net-worth individuals. One of his guiding principles is that if he wouldn't tell his father to invest a certain way, he won't suggest it to his clients. He often suggests options to his clients that mean less commission coming to him in the short-run. But because of this, his clients are incredibly loyal and trusting. The amount of referral business that he gets more than makes up for any commissions or overrides that he loses in the short term. Through up and down markets, his business has always grown. Sales professionals with this approach are playing a game that relies on reputation, relationships, and responsibility.

In many ways, it was easier to be an old-school salesperson. It was definitely simpler. All you had to do was make a ton of calls or knock on a ton of doors until somebody was willing to talk to you. Now, it's important to create relationships and then grow them over time.

Of course, nurturing relationships isn't a new strategy. In many ways it's a natural progression from the solution-based or consultative selling that began to take root around the turn of the century. There's a row of books on my bookshelf that have titles like *High Trust Selling*, *Trustworthy Selling*, *Relationship Selling*, *Spin Selling*, and *The Tao of Sales* that all espouse systems which revolve around this concept of guiding a prospect through their own buying process. This isn't coming out of left field. The difference is, now we don't have a choice. Salespeople need to adopt this method to survive. They can no longer force prospects to work within their sales program, at their pace, and with them in control.

This reinforces the notion that the salesperson isn't going away, but they are changing. Buyers will still engage with the salesperson, but now this occurs farther along in the process. Buyers will have done their research. They'll have visited websites and solicited feedback from their networks. They won't require a salesperson for that. Instead, they need someone to help them process the information. They need help uncovering their real needs. They need guidance in identifying the best solutions to those needs. They need help sorting the valuable data from the noise. And finally, they need to know how to act on their decisions. As a Sales Sherpa, you must be the Morpheus on your prospect's journey.

For experienced salespeople, this mindset shift may seem daunting. It's not as simple or linear as the old way of doing things, because the buyer's journey isn't a straight line anymore. It's rare for a prospect to be sitting and waiting for a call from a sales rep. As we will see in the next chapter, we have to apply different tools and approaches to the sales process because that world of straight lines has been replaced by a complex, three-dimensional grid.

CHAPTER 6

The Linear Sales Process is Dead, Long Live the Sales Matrix™

D o me a favor. Think back to the last book you read on selling. Maybe go to your bookshelf or Kindle library. Pick something at random and scan until you find where the author outlines their sales process. I'd be willing to bet dollars to donuts that the process is a linear one. First you do Step A, then Step B, then you get the prospect to agree to Step C, and then you can close them at Step D. It's simple, it's orderly, and all you have to do is follow the steps for sales success. The only problem: the real world is never as simple as we would like it to be.

> The complexity of the problem, the complexity of the solution, and the complexity of the decision-making process have all increased.

We tell ourselves that the shortest distance between two points is a straight line, but that only holds up if there are indeed just two points: the initial conversation followed by a prospect signing on the dotted line. In the old world of selling, you could get away with looking at the sales process as a straight line because things were a lot simpler. There weren't as many variables. If you were knocking on office doors and selling typewriters, the process was straightforward. But now that same salesperson sells complete office printers that sync with every computer in the office and with the company's other global offices. The complexity of the problem, the complexity of the solution, and the complexity of the decision-making process have all increased.

It's no longer a straight line from beginning to end. When you look at the shape of sales today, you see a ball of relationships and a network of opportunities. It's not shapeless, but it's a 3-D cloud. There are many interconnecting nodes of people and information that we have to plug into. In the Hyper-Connected world, you can think of the sales process as a Sales Matrix™.

A matrix is simply the environment in which something develops. It's the context that surrounds everything. For our purposes, think of the sales matrix as a cloud of inter-connected dots. Each of those dots could be a prospect, a customer, a partner, an influencer, or even someone you don't know who is connected to someone involved in the buying decision. Interspersed with all of these people are pieces of information, decisions, and conversations. The critical aspect of

> **Think of the sales matrix as a cloud of inter-connected dots. Each of those dots could be a prospect, a customer, a partner, an influencer, or even someone you don't know who is connected to someone involved in the buying decision.**

these different nodes: they are all *connected to each other*. They are all in some sort of relationship with each other and with you, and these relationships are constantly changing, shifting, and growing. This is the matrix that defines Hyper-Connected sales.

It's easy to see why some salespeople don't like this new landscape. Straight lines are easier to understand. Complexity requires time and effort, and those are often in short supply. As sales professionals, we are under the same constraints that make our prospects attention-poor. We saw earlier that humans are bad at making decisions with too much information. It makes sense that this would carry over to challenges in understanding complex environments. As statistician Nassim Taleb points out in *Fooled by Randomness*, "Our brain is not cut out for nonlinearities. People think that if, say, two variables are causally linked, then a steady input in one variable should *always* yield a result in the other one. Our emotional apparatus is designed for linear causality."[35]

But oversimplifying how the sales process works today can hurt us. As most salespeople have experienced, the linear "numbers game" of sales tends to crap out right when you're coming up to the end of your sales period. When we mistake the world as being simpler than it really is, we set ourselves up for failure.

The Old-School Sales Funnel

In the old days, many sales processes really *were* more linear than they are today. Where have these processes gone? They're being taken over by computers. It so happens that the older, numbers-based approach to selling is perfectly suited for a processor's logical algorithms. Think about the metaphors that once described the sales process. We would talk about sales *channels*. Or we would call it a sales *pipeline*, which reinforces this idea that everything moves in one direction. Or one of the favorites of sales books: the sales *funnel*. Not only do things move in one direction in a funnel, but there are more inputs in the beginning of the process that get winnowed down as they travel through the funnel.

When you're selling a simple product or service with a relatively low cost, your sales cycle will probably be pretty quick. In these cases, the metaphor of a "funnel" can be useful. The gold standard in many of the older sales industries was the "one-call-close," where the entire sales cycle is encapsulated in a single meeting.

I used to be a manager in home security sales. For us, the goal wasn't to stretch out the sales presentation. We didn't want to come back later for the sale. We walked in with a blank order form and intended to walk out with a completed order form with credit card number or check. In this scenario, there were very few external influences acting on the prospect. They weren't doing outside research, they weren't talking to other people, they weren't spending time and energy mulling over their decision. As the salesperson, your goal was to be the sole supplier of information. We arrived with material that supported our message: everything from crime statistics to competitors' catalogs to stories from happy customers.

This one-call-close sales funnel worked because the product was simple and relatively inexpensive. As we saw in Part I, though, online commerce has largely taken over sales roles for simple, inexpensive products. Ironically, these relatively simple products and services are the most vulnerable to the effects of out-

> **Just like you shouldn't mistake a map for the actual territory, you shouldn't mistake the metaphor of the sales funnel for the actual sales process.**

side influence. When all it takes to shop the competition is another browser window, there are a lot of competing voices that the digital retailer has to worry about. But that's not what we're looking at here, thank goodness.

In the future, we'll continue to see technology and automation take over the sales opportunities that really were linear. Why pay for a salesperson when a well-designed website and online marketing funnel can work the process 24-7, without making mistakes? But for many industries, this linear concept was just a model all along, and like most models, it was an oversimplification. Just like you shouldn't mistake a map for the actual territory, you shouldn't mistake the metaphor of the sales funnel for the actual sales process.

Oversimplifying the sales process had its uses. It can be a convenient way to describe sales to novices. It also gives sales managers a sense of control and authority. If they want to increase the performance of their people, it's just a matter of fine-tuning the linear process. The funnel concept becomes a handy shortcut for controlling a sales team's actions. It was helpful to break out each piece of the process individually to diagnose problems. A sales manager might look at someone's results and say, "Well, Joe, you're horrible at qualifying your leads, so that's why you aren't selling as much we'd like you to." Or you'd hear, "The funnel is perfectly fine, you just need to feed more people into it. How's your cold calling going?"

The sales funnel idea assumes that everyone comes into the pipeline the same way and with the same information. It assumes that prospects enter the program from the same starting point. You would just throw anything or anybody into the top of the funnel, and they would all travel through it the same way. That works if you're starting your sales conversation by cold calling or knocking on doors, or if you're taking inbound leads with a relatively finite amount of information. In these scenarios, the buyer is assumed to have little knowledge and little pre-thought, because they weren't planning on becoming a buyer before they were interrupted. In this context, you use the sales funnel to educate and inform the prospect as well as lead them through the actual sales process.

One of the nice things about having a linear process was that it gave you a checklist for starting, building, and leveraging a sales engagement. When you're following along a straightforward path, you know that you have to check the box for Step #1, then Step #2, then Step #3, etc. Think of this as the "factory-ization" of sales. It allows for anyone to be successful at sales, theoretically. It's why most sales programs and trainers tout their 5-step, or 7-step, or 15-step sales process. If you just follow the program and perform each step, it was assumed that the natural result would be a steady flow of sales.

This approach helped take unskilled and inexperienced employees and make them passable at sales. It sometimes helped top sales-people who liked having a way to think conceptually about how they approached prospects and customers, but mostly the linear sales concept was for new sales reps. A checklist could prevent them from missing important steps, and if a manager looked at their performance, they could see a problem and recommend a solution. Maybe they struggled with asking the right questions to uncover the prospect's pain points. Maybe they didn't know how to ask for the order. Highlighting the step-by-step nature of sales allowed us to complete each segment of the journey. It was just a matter of ticking the boxes.

Even today, people continue to insist that selling is a linear process. Why do this? Simple: linear models are comfortable and convenient. They are easy to grasp. They are the natural end-point of the quantification and attempted "scientification" of sales. It's the physics of sales. If selling can be described by a bunch of numbers in an equation, it's easy to see how our activity will influence our results. And let's be super-honest: The people who have championed this approach are the sales trainers and managers of the world. I include myself in that. Guilty as charged! It gave us a fantastic feeling of control. We could say things like, "We set up appointments 17% of the time when we talk to someone within three days of their initial interest and then we close 54% of our sales calls, so get on the phones today!" When pressed, sales managers will tell you that these numbers aren't very clearly defined as they make them out to be.

In fact, the dirty secret behind these numbers is they aren't actually, well, real. They may seem scientific, but they're mostly guess work. What usually happens is leadership examines the sales results for a set period of time. They take how much business got done, add in some self-reporting from the sales force about their activity (which is almost always off—self-reporting in general is shown to be wildly inaccurate), and plug in guesses for any numbers they don't have. Then they roll them out as if they're gospel. It's a good way to push people to do more and follow the program.

The Hyper-Connected world, of course, has completely wrecked this oversimplified model, or at least thrown it into serious question. By scrapping the linear model and beginning to instead think about a Sales Matrix, we can better understand today's sales process and identify the areas where salespeople will still have the greatest impact.

The Wonderful Complexity of the Sales Matrix

These days, buyers enter your sales process from a number of different starting points. There are those who will be starting cold, in which case they need a lot of initial information. But it's more likely that they're somewhat informed about what you offer and how it connects with their needs. The IDC's 2014 Social Buying Study found that 75% of B2B buyers and 84% of c-suite executives used social media in their decision-making process.[36] When a salesperson enters this situation, they have no idea what the prospect has already learned while surfing through Twitter or LinkedIn. There's an incredibly wide variety of material they might have been exposed to.

In other words, when the sales rep arrives on the scene, the prospect is already at some unknown point in the Sales Matrix. It's important to figure out where the prospect is and meet them there. This requires flexibility and intuition on the part of the sales professional. The prospect might be totally uneducated; on the other hand, they might have all of the latest information at their fingertips.

This is one of the reasons why salespeople who have good question-asking skills will continue to excel. They have the tools to find out where the prospect stands at the beginning of the conversation. From there, the perceptive sales professional can tailor the dialogue to the prospect's needs instead of forcing them into the same cookie-cutter template.

Customized marketing automation attempts to solve a similar problem, but software algorithms aren't going to be as nuanced as humans at interpreting where prospects are in their buying journey. Sales reps are the ones who know how to get prospects on the same page before moving along the sales process.

The ability to assess a prospect's knowledge level isn't important only at the beginning of a sales engagement. Thanks to the constant stream of new information in the Hyper-Connected world, a prospect's sources of information and influence are constantly in flux. As automated, online models take over short-sales cycle products, sales professionals will see sales cycles that are longer and longer, and therefore the Sales Matrix necessarily expands. More and more external influences will need to be factored in. Prospects are going to reach out to colleagues, bosses, competitors, the Internet, and also, YOU, during the course of the buying process.

Remember that seven people, on average, are involved in a buying decision at mid-sized companies. It's rare that the internal champion, the end-user, and the person who green lights the project are all the same person. What if each of these people is checking into three different vendor websites, talking to two friends at the office, and looking at five industry forums on social media? That's seventy additional opportunities for more questions and opinions that must be managed. And the number of people involved in making decisions is actually increasing in many situations.[37]

At any given time, your prospect might send a text to their partner, their colleague, or their friend with a question and get an immediate answer. They can shoot out a quick email to their department heads. They can surf your competitor's website. The prospect is not a static part of the equation. What they know, what they want, and how they're feeling about the process can change in a moment after reading a blog post or receiving a social media message. They are a *variable* variable. They are a variable in flux. As the sales rep, you can kiss control goodbye.

But the dynamic nature of the Sales Matrix opens up opportunities for the savvy sales professionals to distance themselves from the pack. By being responsive and receptive to the prospect, salespeople can stay engaged, continue to influence the buying process, and become even more valuable.

This is why the sales process is becoming more relational than transactional. Many modern sales processes require an ongoing relationship with the prospect. As the salesperson, you need to provide your prospect with information while also managing and framing the interactions they have with other people and other sources of information.

I once attended a speech by Jamie Clarke, a real-life mountaineer who has twice summited Mt. Everest. He explained that there were four base camps up the side of the mountain that served the climbers as they ascended. But the paths between each camp were hardly linear. Each climbing group would take their own route because they had to continuously reassess and adapt their climb. There might be crevasses that opened up, snow storms that made previous paths unpassable, avalanches that could be lethal, and a host of other unexpected events. You can be sure that Clarke had real-life Sherpas along with him on his climbs. The Sherpa people have a wealth of experience about the terrain that helps climbers as they face each unexpected situation. A photo of his Sherpa guides even made it into Clarke's slides.

> **As a Sherpa, you guide prospects through the complex, three-dimensional landscape of today's multi-input buying decisions.**

The complexity of the Sales Matrix is precisely why it's so important for salespeople to embrace their new role as Sales Sherpas. As a Sherpa, you guide prospects through the complex, three-dimensional landscape of today's multi-input buying decisions. Prospects didn't necessarily need a guide back when buying was more of a straight path; but today, they need someone to help them up a mountain that's filled with hidden dangers and unknown variables.

I think of my friend Adam, who is in the financial services business. Every time a major world event happens that could have an impact on his client's investments, he knows they will be assaulted with a wall of information and flat-out noise. He knows that they're watching financial news shows, reading the *Wall Street Journal*, and listening to all the financial "experts" out there. Instead of fighting or hiding from this situation, Adam's goal is to *use* these opportunities. He asks his customers about what they're watching and reading and engages them in a dialogue. He understands that they're working with a lot of information, and he positions himself as a trusted advisor, as their financial Sherpa. It's critical for him to continuously build relationships and provide value.

Moving past the linear sales model doesn't mean the different steps in the sales process aren't important, but it does mean that they're often out of order, or sometimes completely removed from the "sales conversation." Imagine a B2B salesperson sitting down with someone from their network—someone they've been building a relationship with for almost ten years. What would happen if she started the sales conversation with "rapport building" because that's what she learned in sales training? It would be awkward and stilted. They'd already built that rapport. In this scenario, the salesperson would be better-served skipping past the preliminaries and moving to other topics. This would give her more credibility, not less.

The high-pressure sales environments with big action and little transparency are losing their relevance. I don't think they'll disappear overnight, but they're evolving. The industries that ran on high-activity, low-efficiency sales processes are migrating to digital sales. This makes sense. Nobody has to worry about websites having call reluctance or not following the program.

But more complicated products or services continue to need a human touch to sell, and it won't be by a bunch of reps in a boiler room. The sales world is embracing a more nuanced sales cycle, and the way we manage ourselves and others through the sales process is changing as well. By working within the Sales Matrix, we can find success *because* of the complex connectivity of the Hyper-Connected world, not in spite of it.

7

Creating Human Connection

I still remember my first "official" sales call. I was a junior in college and had found a gig that would help pay rent and tuition: selling Cutco knives. I was sitting in Mrs. Campbell's kitchen, ready to run through the presentation I had been learning and rehearsing. I didn't know that I would eventually do thousands of these presentations and teach thousands of other kids how to do them as well. On that day, I was just getting started. I was wet behind the ears and nervous as all get out. I basically had three days of training under my belt, a training manual, and a sample set of knives. It was time to dive in and see what I could do.

I can only imagine how painful it must have been for Mrs. Campbell to listen to me stumble through the sales presentation. It was not pretty. I had zero sales skills. I hadn't learned the fine art of persuasion quite yet. But, after I had read (or bumbled) my way through the presentation, she actually bought something. It hadn't mattered that I wasn't slick and polished, because I had something more important: a human connection.

It also helped that I was working with a quality product, but looking back, what had really cemented this first sale was the relationship I had developed with my prospect—she was my boss from my school-year job. I learned a lesson that day that would impact the rest of my career, because I had seen the power of a relationship in the sales process. Now, Mrs. Campbell hadn't spent hundreds of dollars that day just because she liked me. As I said, it was a quality product, and she needed some new kitchen cutlery. But she was willing to give me a chance and be patient because she already knew me and was willing to trust me.

That interpersonal exchange is at the heart of every sales conversation, and it's the foundation of selling, even in a busy, information-packed, technology-filled world. In fact, especially in a busy, information-packed, technology-filled world. As the more impersonal sales roles are being outsourced to technology and automation, today's salespeople are relearning and embracing the interpersonal relationships that have always been at the core of sales.

> **That interpersonal exchange is at the heart of every sales conversation, and it's the foundation of selling, even in a busy, information-packed, technology-filled world. In fact, especially in a busy, information-packed, technology-filled world.**

The More Things Change...

To fully harness and benefit from the changes happening in the sales world, it's important to firmly acknowledge that sales, and all business relationships, are based on *human* relationships. The better your ability to connect with the person "across the table," the more success you will find in the sales game.

That might not sound revolutionary, but in a world that's becoming more and more technology-driven, paying attention to old-school interpersonal communications skills is too often seen as a radical idea. In truth, the tools required to start and build relationships are just as pertinent as they've always been.

Dale Carnegie came out with *How to Win Friends and Influence People* in 1936, and it's been a perennial favorite with salespeople ever since. Even though we're a few generations down the road, the skills he wrote about not only retain their relevance, they are more important than ever. It would be a mistake to ignore these skills in favor of relying solely on technology solutions. These core competencies continue to drive success, and are becoming increasingly relevant as technology takes jobs away from the order-takers and information-deliverers of yore.

> But in a world that's becoming more and more technology-driven, paying attention to old-school interpersonal communications skills is too often seen as a radical idea.

As these technologies continue to replace many of the routine activities in selling, the one thing that can't be replaced is the human element. There is only so much of the selling process that can be outsourced to a computer. In a world full of marketing automation, sales enablement, and CRM systems, the ability to engage another person is going to remain incredibly valuable. Apps, robots, and algorithms can't empathize. They can't read nuanced body language, and they can't hear subtext or vocal tone to understand when a prospect isn't telling the whole story. As powerful as computers are, the most powerful computer is still the human mind.

In fact, the brains of two people speaking together have been shown to actually sync up with each other.[38] The more layers and variables there are in the sales process, the more it's necessary to have a mind that can handle complexity and uncertainty. After all, that's precisely what human minds have evolved to do.

Moving forward, the top salespeople will be the ones who can create, maintain, and nurture the relationships they have with their prospects, clients, and partners. In a Hyper-Connected environment, honing these skills is one of the easiest forms of career security. As more and more of the transactional, well, transactions are taken care of by technology, the salesperson's role is going to be focused on building relationships with prospects.

And one of the most important things that a Sales Sherpa can provide is trust. If prospects don't trust the person guiding them up the mountain, it's unlikely that they will finish the journey. The human salesperson can create trust in a way that a computer can't. An algorithm can see a pattern in a company's buying decisions, but it can't leverage that information. Give that report to a human salesperson, though, and they can use it to steer conversations and provide value.

It's a pretty standard narrative these days that people have moved beyond the need for these types of human engagement, but that's simply not true. The rising prominence of behavioral economics rests on the realization that humans are still run by their emotions, not by reason.[39] And as the sports science writer David Epstein points out in *The Sports Gene*, our belief that human physical capabilities are growing because we keep breaking world records is misplaced. It's technological improvements in equipment, facilities, and training that allow athletes to perform at higher levels.[40] Humans themselves haven't really changed that much.

Let's take a look at a few critical skills that will rise in prominence in the Hyper-Connected world (and check the resources at the book's website for further reading about building relationships as part of the sales process). There's an old sales adage that is overused and clichéd, but like all clichés, it has the truth at its core. You've probably heard some variation of it: "All things being equal, people will do business with those they know, like, and trust." There's a corollary that can be added: "Even if things aren't that equal, people would *still* rather do business with someone they know, like, and trust."

Building Know, Like, & Trust in the Hyper-Connected World

In later chapters, we will take a deep dive into building sales networks and using social media and digital communication in the selling process. Each and every one of these activities still revolves around building what a sales mentor of mine used to call the Ks, Ls, and Ts: the knows, likes, and trusts in our business interactions.

Starting with the last and most important item on the list, trust is the bedrock of any good sales interaction. Trust is the bridge that connects two people. It's the foundation that the relationship is built on. When we look at structuring our sales efforts, it's worthwhile to pinpoint where we can build trust with prospects and customers.

Humans crave the security that stems from trust, and if you don't believe me, think back to the host of horrible feelings you felt the last time someone betrayed or abused trust in your life. Or think about the prevalence of buyer feedback mechanisms in the online world. A feature that has been on Ebay from the very beginning, for example, is the buyer and seller ratings. The author Rachel Botsman talks about the "trust economy" online, where everything from Airbnb to Uber uses some sort of feedback mechanism allowing people to rate those they interacted with in person.[41] It's been vitally important to translate offline trust into the online world.

> **The Hyper-Connected seller has to work in their prospects' and customers' best interests, because if they don't, others will find out.**

There are numerous resources that analyze how to create trust, but let's face it, the best place to start is by being a trustworthy person. What a concept! The Hyper-Connected seller has to work in their prospects' and customers' best interests, because if they don't, others will find out. It's more important than ever to be a person of your word because there are now more points of contact with others. The effects of our behaviors are magnified. Trust can be lost very fast, sometimes with a single negative review. The big things are important, of course, like being honest about what your products and services can do. But the little things are critical too: being on time to meetings, or responding to messages in a timely fashion.

With trust for salespeople being at a particularly low ebb, what most prospects are looking for is responsiveness and open communication lines. These are small steps that can separate a successful salesperson from an unsuccessful one.[42]

Beyond this foundation, look at how you communicate your trustworthiness in your interactions with others. Think about the list of interpersonal communication skills that you've probably seen before in a sales book. These skills include:

- Creating eye contact
- Using open body language
- Smiling and engaging through facial expressions
- Listening to others without interruption
- Focusing on the person when speaking with them

These might seem obvious, but how good are you at following through with them? How good are you really? Because no matter what tools, techniques, or technologies we put on top of the sales process, in the end, trust comes from connecting with another person and knowing that they have our best interests at heart.

When we have that foundation of trust, we can move to creating the "like." Again, a lot of ink and digital pixels have been used to share how to get people to like you, or love you, or become raving fans of you, or whatever. There's a simple technique, though, that Dale Carnegie wrote about back in the 1930s that still holds sway today: "You can make more friends in two months by becoming interested in other people than you can in two years by trying to get other people interested in you."[43]

People like people who take an interest in them, who let them share, and who value and validate them. So in looking to get people to like you, don't worry about being fascinating or fantastic. Instead, look for opportunities to let them share. Let them create a connection with you. The people you engage with as prospects and customers are probably craving some human attention. They're in the same world as you are, and it's filled with noise and information overload and everyone staring at their smartphones.

I once struck up a conversation with the gentleman sitting next to me during a flight to Texas for a tech conference at Dell Technologies—that's right, not everyone was wearing headphones. He had run a technology reseller for over 20 years and was going to the same conference I was to reconnect with his Dell contacts. That in and of itself shows the importance of continuing to establish human relationships with your business partners. He didn't want to just send an email or shoot over a text. This was one of the biggest technology companies in the world, and yet the human touch was still critical.

We soon started talking about how technology and the sales process were becoming commingled in his firm. He told me that when he interviewed potential salespeople under the age of 30, the first thing he looked for was their cell phone. Was it out? And if it was, was the screen facing up or down?

He wanted to hire someone who understood the importance of engaging with their real-world conversational partners. If someone had their phone out and screen up, he felt they were splitting their attention between him and the phone. If it was out but the screen was down, they were on the right path. But if the phone wasn't there at all, he felt they were focused entirely on the conversation. When asked where his phone was, one of the candidates said, "Well, I'm in an interview, so I thought it made sense to put my phone away." This is the same candidate who eventually got the job.

Engaging with the person you're currently talking to is a very simple concept, but lack of offline engagement has become a real problem. For the younger generations who were exposed to multiple screens from day one, we don't yet fully know what the effects will be. Technology has evolved, but our basic human need for interaction hasn't changed one bit. People's feelings still get hurt when they're being ignored.

In her books *Alone Together* and *Reclaiming Conversation*, renowned Harvard psychologist Sherry Turkle points to a worrying empathy gap in face-to-face communication.[44] She points out that it's making people unhappy and less productive. At the same time, though, futurists point to the benefits of growing up in an environment that is bigger and more connected than ever before. The truth is, no one knows what the long term effects of these monumental changes in the nature of daily interactions will be. But we do know that at least in the near future, humans aren't going to lose their need to connect with the people they do business with.

But let's dispense with the idea that younger people are inherently bad at in-person communication because they grew up surrounded by technology. Of course technology has influenced them. It's been omnipresent in their life, and it's not because they are stupid, lazy, or distracted. It's simply because part of their life has always been lived digitally. The younger generation of salespeople might not have as much experience in face-to-face interactions, or at least deliberate training in face-to-face interactions, but they have a leg up in a lot of other areas instead. For example, they're good at long-term relationship-building in online contexts, like social media. There's a give and take to growing up in a world where online communication is an inherent part of the mix.

No matter your age, there are many ways to improve offline communication skills in ways that will enhance and complement online communication skills. The solution that Sherry Turkle sees is a simple one: engage in more in-person conversations. Screens aren't a final death sentence to our interpersonal communication skills. If you want to improve these skills, practice them. And if you don't feel comfortable with where your current skills are at, create new opportunities for practice. It's a good thing you're in a sales position, because you have a great excuse to do just that.

Which brings us to the last leg of the Ks, Ls, and Ts: Know. How do you get someone to know you? More importantly, how do you get someone to know you when, as we have already established, the best way to make someone like you is to let *them* talk?

First of all, just because you're focused on someone else doesn't mean that you're going to be mute. Normal human interaction involves a high degree of reciprocity, so if you're truly focusing on your conversational partner, it will become natural for them to want to ask about you in return. This is part of the ideal give-and-take of a good conversation.

It's important to focus on how you might answer these conversational questions before you're even asked. The "know" part of the equation actually happens well before you start the conversation. Getting someone to know you should be simple, so long as you're comfortable with yourself and practice describing yourself to others. In other words, letting other people know about us requires us to first know ourselves.

It's important that we are clear and concise when we tell other people about ourselves, especially in a professional environment. We have to define in advance what we're really all about: who our customers are, how we help them, why we help them, what makes us tick as individuals, and what we're passionate about. If you think about these qualities in advance, when the topic comes up, it's easy for us to share.

This is the first place I'm going to mention your personal brand, but it won't be the last. It is critical to be clear about who you are and how you show up in your sales interactions. And once you have that knowledge firmly in place, you'll be able to engage with your prospects, clients, and overall network in a genuine and effective manner.

When you look at the power of social media and technology, one of its most useful benefits is the ability to build this know, like, and trust with a wider audience. But before you establish your brand on a larger scale, you need to know yourself and be willing to convey your true self in a one-on-one, face-to-face conversation.

If you can't have a simple conversation that builds your relationship with another person, you're going to struggle to find a place in the Hyper-Connected sales world, because everything is an extension of that conversation.

True, the rise of online communication has been beneficial for people who aren't as strong at offline interactions, and that's great. But even for those people, improving offline communication skills will benefit and augment their online abilities. When people ask me about specific scenarios that they encounter on LinkedIn, I usually ask, "Well, what would you do in the offline world?" The solution is usually close at hand when they think of it that way.

I once had someone pose a question about following up with a college friend for a job recommendation. The asker had someone in their network they had attended school with almost twenty years ago and who now worked for a company she wanted to approach for a position. She wanted to know if she could contact her friend out of the blue and ask for an introduction to a hiring manager. My guidance was simple: "If you didn't have access to social media, and you ran into this person at a reunion, what would you do?" She said she would ask for the introduction, but would be sure to give her contact a graceful way out if it wasn't possible to help. And with that, she had answered her own question.

No matter the ways that we use technology, we still have to connect with people as people. It's not that I'm digging my heels in and saying that we have to go old-school for old-school's sake. It's because powerful things happen when we can engage with other people as people. When we build on this foundation, all of the other pieces of the Hyper-Connected sales process will work so much more smoothly.

8

Asking for the Next Step™

If you could develop a robot to take over one aspect of the sales process, what would it do? Would you want it to make your phone calls for you, go through your sales presentation, or survey the customer to find their pain points?

My guess is a lot of salespeople would want to outsource one of the most challenging parts of the sales interaction: asking for commitment. Whether you call it "closing," "asking for the order," or "getting the OK," the act of asking a prospect to become a customer is one of the most

> Everything before and after gains meaning at the moment a salesperson says, "Would you like to go ahead with this?"

stressful parts of the sales process. Prospecting takes a lot of time, sales presentations take skill, but asking for business requires vulnerability. It's where all of the possibilities that you've developed can become realized. It's also where the prospect can say no and bring the whole matter to an end.

Going back to the ideas that we explored in Part I, selling is all about creating something new. It's about connecting a solution to a problem. Everything before and after gains meaning at the moment a salesperson says, "Would you like to go ahead with this?"

It's the pivot point that the whole process revolves around. Prospecting leads up to it, and the delivery and follow-up stem from it. It's the most important point of the process, and is the core of the sales job. That's a lot of pressure on a small part, a mere moment among the overall interaction with a prospect, and not everyone responds well to that pressure. Teeing up the prospect to say yes or no can be pretty nerve-wracking.

For sales reps who hate that lead-up to closing, the Hyper-Connected environment has something new to offer. Instead of thinking of sales as leading to a single closing moment, we can think of multiple moments during the journey that all move the process forward. Instead of "closing," I like to call this asking for the Next Step™.

Goodbye to Closing, Hello to the Next Step™

Don't get me wrong. The skills and emotional fortitude necessary to being a good "closer" are still incredibly valuable for the Hyper-Connected seller. Indeed, the ability to ask questions that drive the relationship forward are even more important. Asking for the business will always be a key component of a salesperson's job description. If it wasn't needed, then the job would be outsourced to a website or app.

In the non-linear Sales Matrix, *asking* becomes a key tool in guiding prospects and customers through the sales cycle. But what we ask for shifts. Relationships unfold over time instead of at the moment of closing. A key part of long-term prospecting is asking for all of the little actions and agreements that build and strengthen the relationship. And most importantly, knowing how to ask the types of questions that move the relationship and sales process forward.

Since the Sales Matrix isn't a simple step-by-step process, there are multiple paths forward. We can't point to a specific place in the process called "Ask for the Order." There are a lot of ways to get to the finish line, and many possible detours and roundabouts you might go through to get there. Your job as a Sales Sherpa is to move the conversation forward without a predefined map. Some sales reps dislike this uncertainty and others thrive on it, but whichever you are, you need to embrace it, because Hyper-Connected sellers don't ask for the order. They ask for the Next Step.

The Next Step might be asking if the prospect would like to become a client, but it also might be a different, earlier step. It might mean sending an invitation on LinkedIn. It might mean asking to meet for a cup of coffee. It might mean asking to visit their office for a sales presentation. It's important to know how to read the prospect and predict which step they'll be most comfortable with. There are a lot of paths through the Sales Matrix, and the only way that a salesperson can guide a prospect through the process is if the prospect is actually moving. Asking questions is how to keep moving people through their journey

Let's use the analogy of dating. Imagine it's a Friday night at the local singles bar, the "meet/meat" market where packs of single men and women mingle in the hopes of finding Mr. or Mrs. Right, or even Mr. and Mrs. Right Now. You probably know of a few of these places, either from your past or because you're going to one with your friends next weekend. I always found them interesting because every night they're filled with sales and networking conversations. (I'm a bit of a nerd that way. I just can't turn off the sales coach part of my brain.) If you pay attention, there is prospecting happening, referrals being asked for, value-building… the whole shebang.

More than anything, there's a lot of "asking." It might be asking if you can sit next to someone at the bar, asking for their phone number, or even asking if they want to get out of there to get a drink somewhere else. Everyone knows what their end goal is, and they know there's not a clear-cut path to get there.

In this environment, what would happen if you asked someone to marry you after talking to them for five minutes? That would never work. It's totally inappropriate. It makes sense to ask someone for their phone number the first time you meet them. It doesn't make sense to ask them to marry you. You have to go through the full dating process, which is full of relationship-building, question-asking, and value-creation.

Moving this back to sales, think about what happens when you try to close the sale at the wrong time. It's important to recognize where you are in the sales conversation, and what the appropriate next step would be to move the conversation forward. If this sounds like a complicated pro-

> We can't make the mistake of thinking the real world is going to conform to our step-by-step sales diagrams and simplistic processes.

cess, that's because it is. We can't make the mistake of thinking the real world is going to conform to our step-by-step sales diagrams and simplistic processes. There are a lot of moving parts in the Sales Matrix. There are a lot of starts and stops, even little ones.

But we should be happy for this level of interpersonal complexity and unpredictability, because it's what's keeping our profession relevant. Technology and automation are good for when you know all of the possibilities, but what happens when something totally unexpected happens? It's important to have the skills to go with the flow and follow the needs of the engagement.

In the old days, a sales rep knew exactly why they were having every conversation and what they were supposed to get at the end of it. That's the power of a linear sales model. Every conversation had a clear finish line. They knew that their goal was to get a sale; to have someone sign on the dotted line. If a sales rep was talking with a prospect, the focus of their conversation was to build value and ask for the order when the time was right—and then handle any objections or rejections. If a rep was making cold calls, their job was to get the decision-maker on the phone and book the appointment. If the rep was at a networking event or an industry conference, their goal was to make sure every conversation was focused on determining whether someone was a prospect and getting their information if they were. This is why salespeople developed a reputation for looking over your shoulder at networking events to see if there was someone else they should be talking to.

I remember an early conversation I had with someone about social selling. In fact, it was early enough that nobody was calling it social selling yet. This was around 2010, back when we were still figuring out how to use all the new digital and social media platforms for sales purposes. I was talking with an old-school sales rep who was practically shouting, "This social media for selling is bullshit! Nobody will close a deal because someone Twittered them." Even then, my response was, "Of course not. But that's like saying you aren't going to close a deal because you call a prospect on the phone." It's not about the medium, it's about keeping the message appropriate to the context.

> One of the most valuable skills to develop today is "situational awareness"—understanding which tools to use in which situations.

My point was, it's obvious that digital platforms won't replace every part of the sales interaction. It isn't a magic pill that makes people automatically buy from you, and you won't usually close with a tweet or LinkedIn InMail. But getting that closing commitment is only a short part of the process. One of the most valuable skills to develop today is "situational awareness"—understanding which tools to use in which situations. Closing is a part of the sales process that still usually works best in-person or during a phone conversation, so don't hide behind your screen when you're asking for the business. But at the same time, we have a lot of valuable tools in our kits today, and we shouldn't throw one out just because we don't always use it during the closing conversation.

There's nothing wrong with having goal-focused conversations. Frankly, many business communications and conversations would be better if a specific focus was more clearly defined. Many of us have been to too many meetings where nobody is sure what the end result should be. So the point isn't about the existence of a clear goal. A salesperson's goal, as we discussed in Part I, is still clear: creating the sale. We should still know exactly where we want to end up. But in today's world, we need to be more flexible about how we're going to get there.

Techniques for Moving the Relationship Forward

I learned some great lessons about sales while in an unlikely environment: the improv comedy stage. I was never going to be a cast member on SNL, but living in Chicago, you're surrounded by great improv institutions. I liked to dabble. In my classes I learned to find a balance between having a goal and being flexible as to how you would get there. As one of the master improv teachers, Patricia Ryan Madson, once wrote, "An improvisation always has a point. It is never simply a "whatever"... some guiding force underlies each moment. We need to keep in mind what we are aiming for."[45] So even in improv comedy—an art form that's by definition scriptless—it's important to know where you're going.

> **During your sales engagements, you should keep the end goal of the sale in mind, but be open to how you will get the customer to that point.**

During your sales engagements, you should keep the end goal of the sale in mind, but be open to how you will get the customer to that point. This is part of why critical thinking and creativity are crucial skills for the Hyper-Connected salesperson. We have to learn how to see opportunities that are hidden or need to be created from scratch. Not only are we asking for the Next Step to move the conversation along, but we often need to come up with the Next Step on the fly. Sometimes the Next Step is something unexpected, like sharing an idea that another client had with your prospect, or maybe it's asking the right question to help the prospect clarify what they really need or want. Whatever the particulars, it's safe to say that the Next Step is usually a far cry from what the order-takers of the past were doing.

Think of this as a real-life *Choose Your Own Adventure* novel. I read these all the time when I was younger, and I might have cheated a bit. I would look through the books and find all of the pages with the "bad" endings where you got caught by the bad guys or dropped off a cliff. Then, as I went through the book, I'd be sure to not pick choices that landed on those pages. But I'd eventually get stymied by trying to remember how I got to where I was. I realized there were a lot of ways to go through the book, and I just had to try again if I didn't get what I wanted the first time. Whenever I tried to hold on too tightly to the ending that I wanted, I would invariably get stuck. I still knew what I wanted the ideal ending to be, but I had to learn to be flexible with how I would be getting there.

The Sales Matrix paradigm creates an open format that a salesperson can use to move the relationship forward. There's a bit of a paradox here, because even though the process isn't linear, we're still trying to create momentum that is going in one direction. We're just being open to the fact that it could happen in many different ways.

We can break this down by looking at different parts of the sales interaction. In the prospecting phase alone, there are many junctures where an important Next Step question might be relevant. Asking for the Next Step during prospecting might include:

- Asking for a business card at the networking reception at a conference
- Asking for a 15-minute introductory phone call
- Asking for an introduction to someone the customer knows
- Asking if you can do a sales presentation
- Asking if you can introduce them to someone they might want to know

- Asking to stay in touch on social media
- Asking to connect on LinkedIn
- Asking to set up another coffee meeting in 3 months to stay in touch
- Asking if you can add them to your e-newsletter list

There are a number of possibilities during the prospecting phase, and each of those might have different branches of possibility that follow from them.

Later in the process, when we get to actual sales conversations, getting the business can have a lot of different looks and feels in the Hyper-Connected landscape. Indeed, the concept of "closing" itself has altered significantly in recent years. In the linear process that used to define sales, closing was a finite moment that happened once. It's step #_____ in the process. When I first learned the Cutco sales presentation, there was exact verbiage that I learned, on page 10 of the training manual, to ask for the order. It went like this:

"Mr. and Mrs. Jones, I wouldn't be doing my job if I didn't ask, would you like to go ahead and place an order for that cutlery set today entitling yourself to the free kitchen tools and super shears?" In a simple, step-by-step process, it's just a matter of inserting the right question at the right place and letting the prospect answer. There were/are books filled with potential closing questions that are designed to get the prospect to say yes all the time. At least that's what the titles claim.

But remember, if it's really that simple and basic, it's going to be taken over by technology. This is what we're seeing with online marketers. If Amazon or an AI-driven automated marketing campaign can get someone's credit card with a simple question, that's where the business will go. So that's not where humans are going to be making their mark. Moving forward, we can expect that the types of "closing" situations that humans will be an integral part of will lean to the side of complexity.

In the Sales Matrix, no longer is asking for the business a one-time occurrence. When there are multiple variables, decision-makers, and steps to move through, it makes sense that there will be many opportunities to ask for something. Because of this, the word "closing" is ceasing to be a valuable way of looking at the process. It denotes something that happens at the end of the process, at the "close" of the conversation. Closing in the modern world can and should happen all along the journey.

Sales will continue to be more of a negotiation than a one-off question. And these different opportunities to ask for the Next Step will not necessarily be at clearly-defined points in the process. One of the biggest hurdles salespeople face with open-ended conversations is that there isn't always an easily-defined endpoint to focus on, and for some, that makes the conversation stressful. They would rather be in a sales meeting and think to themselves, "My purpose here is to set up a moment where I can ask for the sale. I want to walk out of this meeting with a commitment to buy."

And that might work when the prospect is truly ready for a buying conversation. But what if you're jumping into that too early? What if you misread the situation? As we saw earlier, paying attention to the context is critical, because then you can connect the Next Step question with the ideal next phase in the process. Rather than asking for the buy, the appropriate question might be asking for a follow-up meeting. It might be asking to bring in another person to help make the decision, and yes, it still might be asking for the commitment to buy.

Moving the prospect through this process is one of the ways that today's salesperson creates something new. And it's also how they can add their particular brand of creativity. I recently had an interesting conversation with Sarah Thurber, author of *The Secret of the Highly Creative Thinker: How To Make Connections Others Don't.*[46] She's also the CEO of Foursight Analytics, a company that assesses creativity in individuals and organizations. In Foursight's model, creativity has four proficiencies: Ideation, Clarification, Development, and Implementation. Some people excel more at one stage or another, but all of them are necessary for the successful execution of a project.

Thurber pointed out that there's a natural ebb and flow to the process. "First, you have a lot of ideas, and then you narrow those down," she said. "Then you clarify the winners to make sure they're the right path to pursue. Once that's been agreed to, you can move from there to development and implementation. It's all about expanding the ideas, and then focusing on the best course of action for execution."

During our conversation, I realized that this process is very similar to what occurs within the Sales Matrix. Where a Hyper-Connected salesperson excels is not in a specific individual segment, but in linking each of these steps together. They move the process along. A salesperson is the quarterback in this scenario, always assessing the situation, giving instructions, and moving people toward the goal line.

The final step of asking for the business is just one piece in an open format. There will even be Next Steps that happen after asking for and getting the business. The Hyper-Connected salesperson isn't going to disappear once they get a signed contract. Not at all. After the sale has been made, additional Next Steps might include:

- Confirmation about delivery
- Introductions to others who are responsible for implementation
- Feedback on how the process went for the customer
- Testimonials to share with future potential customers
- Recommendations to other internal and external prospects

Successful salespeople in the Hyper-Connected world always have the long view in mind, and what happens *after* the order continues to impact a customer's satisfaction and therefore a salesperson's reputation. It's important to stick around well after the business is closed to make sure that implementation went smoothly. And in industries with longer or more complex delivery processes after the sale, social media has become a fantastic tool for keeping in touch with clients during and after delivery.

The rising importance of the continuous, non-linear Next Step process signifies the end of the concept of "closing." A truly fundamental shift in the nature of what salespeople are asking for has occurred. In the linear sales paradigm of the old days, there were specific times and places to ask for specific, clearly-defined actions. You asked for the initial sales conversation, then you asked for an opportunity to present a proposal or give a demo, and then you asked for the order. Each of these was a big deal. Without a positive response, the conversation was stalled or over forever. If someone said "no," you moved on to the next prospect.

But in the Sales Matrix, the act of asking is the linkage between each node in the process. It gives you permission to continue the conversation. Your main job as a salesperson in this novel landscape is to keep things moving forward, and this is something that humans are uniquely suited for because we understand context better than computers do.

Your goal as a Sales Sherpa is to make sure your prospects and clients keep moving up that mountain. They might not be able to see the peak just yet. Maybe they're way back at the mountain's base, not yet ready to start the ascent. In that case, you want to keep things warm and moving. Then, when it's time to make a bigger ask, they're ready for it. The important thing is to always be asking the right question, because if you remain attuned to the situation, the bigger question will be right around the corner.

9

Drive: The Human Element

I have a distinct memory of sitting in a hotel ballroom as a young sales manager, listening to one of the top managers in the organization go through the fundamental success metrics for our salespeople. He was walking through the KPIs, the key performance indicators, that we needed to track so that we could help our people be successful.

He looked at a number of categories, including closing percentages, average order size, number of appointments, etc. But all of those led back to one metric that he exhorted us to know every day. More importantly, he said, we should be totally focused on *increasing* it every day: the number of phone calls our sales team made to set up appointments. He went so far as to say that if we tracked only one number, it should be these calls. Everything in the organization boiled down to that. The more activity on the phones, the more we would sell.

And so I spent a lot of my time as a sales manager trying to figure out how to increase the amount of activity that my sales team could generate. Whether it was learning how to motivate each person on an individual basis, or putting systems and processes in place to make it easier and more efficient, my life revolved around getting sales reps to do more. We had to constantly motivate them because they were doing hard work. Not hard work like digging ditches, but hard emotional work because they were dealing with rejection. And as humans, we are wired to hate even hearing the word "no".

This is something that's built into our genetics and reinforced in our childhoods. We hate being rejected. I remember watching a sales rep stare at the telephone for an hour instead of making a phone call to set up an appointment. He was a talented and successful rep, but he sometimes psyched himself out of approaching new clients because he was afraid of hearing the "no." We had to focus on always pushing our people past that mental block.

In the new Hyper-Connected landscape, success is less about these types of numbers. It's not as much about facing rejection over and over again on a daily basis. But rejection is still part of the game, and selling still requires that certain type of tenacity that I like to call drive.

The Elusive Quality of Drive

As we saw when looking at the evolution of sales cultures, the aggressive culture of the gatecrashers didn't pop up out of thin air. It was focused on helping salespeople manage the emotionally challenging aspects of selling so that they would keep trying. In this context, activity was the most important guide for success, and everything had to focus on getting a salesperson to make one more attempt than they usually would.

If you look at the books available to salespeople, most are focused on helping them create more activity. Think of the parade of motivational speakers going through the sales conference circuit. The reason they're there? To motivate you to do more work. Even books like this one, which aren't specifically geared towards motivating you to a specific activity, have an underlying theme of action—my hope is that you will leverage your knowledge of

Hyper-Connected selling to engage in highly-effective "connecting" activities.

Given our focus on motivating salespeople to action, it seems like being active must be pretty important! Indeed, it is. If the main way to create success is to get in front of as many people as possible, it makes sense to get in front of as many people as possible. For years, the sales world was run by the idea of "the numbers game." If you knew that for every ten calls you made, three people would set up a sales presentation, and of those three people, one would buy, then you could work backward to find out how many calls you needed to make to hit whatever sales goal you had. You could look at the sales equation as having three parts: Number of attempts x success % = number of sales.

> **Selling in the Hyper-Connected world demands just as much, if not more, activity than selling did only a few years ago. It requires creative energy to reach out, start relationships, and move them along. It also requires the creativity to put that activity in the context of an environment that is evolving rapidly.**

Your success ratio, or closing percentage, was capped at 100%. You could never be better than that, but there was no cap on how many attempts you could make. And because the closing percentage was rarely 100%, these attempts were inevitably made in an environment where sales reps constantly dealt with rejection and its emotional consequences.

This is why the motivational style in sales was like a brute instrument to make people keep moving forward. There wasn't a lot of self-reflection in sales. It was about picking up the phone again or knocking on another door or saying hello to one more receptionist. If you're a gatecrasher, your job is to crash as many gates as possible. It's why the sales world abounds with aphorisms like Wayne Gretzky's "You miss 100% of the shots you never take!" and Michael Jordan's famous "I have failed over and over and over again...and that is why I succeed."

Today, we don't want to lose that drive, but we do want to reframe it. Selling in the Hyper-Connected world demands just as much, if not more, activity than selling did only a few years ago. It requires creative energy to reach out, start relationships, and move them along. It also requires the creativity to put that activity in the context of an environment that is evolving rapidly. It's still important to know how to make a prospecting phone call, compose a professional email, or start a conversation at a networking event, but now it's also important to know when to do each of these. Having the insight to apply the correct activity at the correct time is becoming an incredibly valuable ability.

> Having the insight to apply the correct activity at the correct time is becoming an incredibly valuable ability.

Hyper-Connected salespeople must continue to be the drivers behind their own self-motivated activity. By capturing the dynamic elements of the old-school sales energy and refining it for a new environment, the Hyper-Connected salesperson becomes even more irreplaceable. Drive is as critical as ever.

> By capturing the dynamic elements of the old-school sales energy and refining it for a new environment, the Hyper-Connected salesperson becomes even more irreplaceable. Drive is as critical as ever.

Nassim Taleb, one of the leading thinkers on the effects of randomness and non-linear processes in business, points out that as the world has become more complicated, putting in effort is still important, but in a different way. Hard work is still necessary. But now, it's not always a *sufficient* cause for success, which means that the game is now harder, not easier.[47] Too often, the critics of the new world see the nuance of something like the Sales Matrix as an excuse for laziness. To the contrary. Sustained effort remains a critical ingredient in the sales success recipe.

When we talk about a salesperson's activities today, though, we are expanding beyond just making phone calls or other prospecting activities. As we've already established, if it was just about doing a routine activity over and over, it would be outsourced to technology. This is why we have robo-dialers doing all of the actual calling in call centers, and then connecting a human when someone picks up the phone. It's why there's that pause before a telemarketer starts talking and why I hang up immediately if I pick up the phone and hear silence.

Sales is inherently creative, and what it takes to create the sale is different now. It's about balancing a host of options when engaging with new and existing relationships. Whether this is called drive, ambition, energy, or hustle, sales professionals can't sit still. Sales is about movement, and the nature of the movement has changed. We can't continue to do the same activities that we always did in the same way we always did them. We can't go through the motions and wait for business to come. There has rarely been a place for passivity in sales, and the Hyper-Connected world will heighten that. If the buyer's journey is evolving, it makes sense that the salesperson's journey is evolving right along with it. The ability to make new connections and find new solutions is a necessity.

The Boundless Activity of Salespeople

In 2015, Forrester Research, a leading market research company, published a study of sales organizations that differentiated between four archetypes seen in sales roles.[48] First are the *Order-takers* and *Explainers* working in environments where there isn't a lot of complexity in the buyer dynamic. These are roles that will be subsumed by technology as a matter of digital transformation. *Navigators*, while having a name that sounds like our Sales Sherpa, work well in environments where there is a complex buyer dynamic, but not a lot of complexity in the product or service. The fourth category, the *Consultants*, are the individuals who sell complex products and services in a complicated buyer's environment.

Basically, these are the Sales Sherpas consulting with prospects who are going through the Sales Matrix. Today, and even more so in the future, these consultants will be in high demand. According to the Forrester report, order-takers, explainers, and navigators are losing their jobs, while consultants are actually being hired. "The way salespeople can save their jobs is by becoming consultants," the report concludes.

To be a successful consultative seller, you can't be passive. You can't wait for the prospect to come to you with their challenges. You have to go to them. Companies can outsource the passive components of the sales role to a website or an app, so salespeople are being paid for the work that can't be outsourced. This includes: creativity, enthusiasm, ambition, drive, desire, and a host of other emotions that generate forward movement.

Going back to the vital role that phone calls once played in sales, think about how everything else was predicated on making those calls. If you didn't have a prospect to talk to, the rest of your sales process was moot. Jerry Otteson, a legend in the Cutco business and one of the first motivational speakers I ever saw, used to shout from the stage, "If you aren't in front a prospect, you're unemployed!" After all, it didn't matter if you closed 100% of your sales calls if you didn't have any to begin with. And so it was easy to know if you were working hard—you simply looked at your call sheet. This is why the saying, "Plan your work and then work your plan" was so popular. There was no reason to complicate success. You just had to show up and do the work for the day.

But if you're a Sales Sherpa, it's not as simple. On any given day, your activity could include:

- Following up with existing prospects by email after a sales demo
- Sharing relevant industry news online
- Answering a question from a networking connection

- Running a sales demo by video conference
- Analyzing your pipeline to see which marketing strategies are working

And of course, there will always be a lot of prospecting in your day. But it won't necessarily involve you, a telephone, and a list of people. Sometimes it will. Your prospect list might be full of inbound leads that your marketing team gave you that are totally qualified and ready to go. More than likely, though, you need to research your prospects before contacting them. Or you might be developing your own list by using online tools like LinkedIn to make sure that you're talking to the right people about the right topics. Maybe your prospecting involves going to a conference or event because you got the attendee list beforehand and were able to research who should be on your "hit list." Or maybe you're talking to existing customers for referrals. Nowadays, your daily activity plays out in many different ways.

When I talk to established (and usually older) sales professionals about what sales activity looks like in the Hyper-Connected world, I typically get two types of responses. One is subtly (or sometimes overtly) hostile. I hear the echoes of the aggressive sales cultures of the past saying that anything less than banging your head against a wall is weak and lacks value. It's the sales equivalent of your dad telling you, "In my day, we walked five miles to school uphill both ways…in the snow…with no shoes…"

These sales reps have convinced themselves that if you aren't banging out the hard, emotionally taxing work that they once did, then you aren't worthy of being a salesperson. Well, I'm here to tell you that's bullshit. It's just one generation complaining about the next, and it's always been this way. Heck, 2,500 years ago Plato quoted Socrates as saying, "The children now love luxury. They have bad manners, contempt for authority; they show disrespect for elders and love chatter in place of exercise." So maybe we should take these grumblings with a bit of salt.

The other response I typically get is, "Well, yeah. That's what I've been doing for years." It wasn't always talked about around the conference room table, but a lot of top salespeople were working as Hyper-Connected sellers well before the world was Hyper-Connected. I have a friend who had a career as a top seller for CDW, regularly appearing in the top ten among the hundreds and hundreds of salespeople there. He was often tapped to train the new recruits to help them develop the sales skills that had propelled him to success. This consisted of a lot of the old-school sales tactics that we've talked about: hit the phones, follow up relentlessly, ask for the order, etc.

But over dinner one night, I asked him where he got his business from during his best stretches. He said that he had a handful of accounts he had grown over the years. He had built relationships with the key decision-makers and was always looking for ways to help them with their technology needs. The amount that these accounts spent with him and CDW grew every year. In the parlance, he had started as a Hunter who was constantly looking for new targets. But over time, he had evolved into a Farmer, cultivating a patch of customers who would take care of him just like he took care of them.

We'll look again at Hunting and Farming in a later chapter about networking, but what's important to understand is that successful salespeople intuitively know that being a Hunter requires a lot of work. At some point they realize that they will get better long-term returns by putting the same amount of effort into being a Farmer.

If you have ever met a farmer, you know that the work ethic involved puts even the most dedicated salesperson to shame. Farmers put in the effort because they don't have a choice. If they don't take care of their fields and their animals, there won't be a payoff at the end of the season. In the same way, selling in the Hyper-Connected world necessitates a high level of commitment. It's not about cutting corners or being lazy. It's about drive. It's about constantly responding to the prospect's needs. And as we're about to see, it involves networking at an advanced level.

PART III

Working the Networking

10

Creating Access and Opportunity

L et's paint a picture:

It's a Tuesday night at about 6:30. You've had a full day of client work, meetings, and emails. You would like nothing better than to go home, grab some time with the family, and relax a little before doing it all again tomorrow. Instead you're at a local restaurant, in the back room, listening to someone who you are rapidly realizing doesn't have a job and is looking for one. And did I mention the lukewarm appetizers?

Ah, networking.

This is the idea that many of us have in mind when we think about networking. Networking has always occupied this interesting space both in our own minds and in the business culture at large. It's the most extreme of love/hate relationships.

I've been writing and speaking about networking for years. When I tell people that, they react in one of two ways. The overwhelming majority (like 99%) groan and go, "I really don't like to network. I know I should do it more, but I just don't like it." The other sliver is filled with the networking obsessives who will tell you how strong and wide their network is within 15 seconds of meeting you. These are usually the same people that make the other 99%

hate it. They view it as a numbers game, and they pass their business card out to as many people as possible.

It's time to shift our relationship with networking, and the best way to start is to redefine it. Instead of seeing networking as just another prospecting tool, we can view it as an integrated part of the Sales Matrix. In the Hyper-Connected world, networking is about much more than getting a business card and eating free nachos. In the broader life cycle of our professional relationships, networking is what allows us to get into

> **Instead of seeing networking as just another prospecting tool, we can view it as an integrated part of the Sales Matrix.**

the door of a sales conversation without having to get past the gatekeepers. Networking is effective because it gets you inside while nobody's paying attention to keeping you out. And in the Hyper-Connected world, there are more ways than ever to go about networking. You might even begin to enjoy it.

The Network is Everywhere

When done right, networking isn't its own separate activity. It should connect to everything else that you're doing. In some ways, networking is a sort of overlay that encompasses the entire Sales Matrix. What is a network but a group of highly-connected nodes? What is the Sales Matrix but people and information that are connected to each other? Seen in this light, networking activities comprise a concrete way of moving through the Hyper-Connected environment.

Let's get away from thinking of a business card exchange at a conference cocktail reception as the total sum of what networking is. That interaction is just a small piece of the puzzle, and it's where many salespeople get stuck. They think that networking is just another way to feed their sales pipeline. As my friend Brian Hilliard, co-author of *Networking Like a Pro*, puts it, "Too many people approach networking as in-person cold-calling. If that's your approach you are going to fail, and be miserable while doing so."[49]

Many salespeople still think of networking as an alternative to going through a list of prospects by phone or email. They approach networking with the goal of talking to as many people as possible in a room to see if they can find a potential lead. That doesn't work well, and we already know why. It treats something that should be relational as transactional, and that cheapens it.

We've all been on the receiving end of that sort of approach. We've been at a conference or a business event and had a salesperson approach us and begin to feel us out right away. We have their business card within three seconds, and they start asking qualifying questions right out of the gate. They're continually looking over our shoulder to see who they should hit up next. There's an online version of this, too. It's when you say "yes" to a LinkedIn connection request, then get a sales pitch right back within minutes. Nobody likes being viewed as an opportunity and nothing more.

We tend to think about our network and networking activities as a way to drive business, but that approach is less successful than it used to be. Modern networking is about much more than finding prospects. Many of the Next Step activities we mentioned in the last chapter are networking activities, and they happen outside of a formal sales conversation. And when we examined the buyer's journey in Part I, we saw that a lot of the buying process is now happening before buyers officially engage with a salesperson. In these new contexts, networking can be used to help salespeople with two important activities in the Hyper-Connected landscape.

> **Modern networking is about much more than finding prospects.**

First, salespeople need to ensure that their company is being considered in the preliminary research portion of the buyer's journey. It's important to get on the radar of the customer when they're first creating their list of potential vendors. It's hard to get the nod when you're not even on the list of options. Secondly, salespeople need to ensure that they're getting the call when the prospect goes from researching to decision-making. The salesperson wants to be top of mind at that all-important moment and positioned as the go-to expert. You might not be the only person they call, but you want to be on the short list.

The salesperson should use a variety of networking activities to make sure they're on the radar of the decision-makers, and that they've been supplying valuable support all along. The real value of this pre-sales contact and networking is all about <u>positioning</u>. When a salesperson consistently provides high-quality information and advice via networking and pre-sales activities, they are creating a connection in prospects' minds about their level of expertise.

The goal of today's sales rep is to position themselves as the go-to expert in their field. We'll explore this more in the next chapter, when we discuss personal branding. Whether the prospect is a married couple deciding to buy a new home, an entrepreneur deciding which graphic designer to hire, or a project committee deciding which payroll software to use, the salesperson wants to become the natural person for them to call when they need help.

Planting and Cultivating Seeds

In the old paradigm, salespeople looked at their network as a resource to "tap-into" at best, or "plunder" at worst. In contrast, the Hyper-Connected sales professional views their network as a field of opportunity where they are growing future sales. Modern networking is all about planting and cultivating seeds.

Top salespeople realize that they fit into a broader landscape. The more they can connect and provide value to the people in their network, the better positioned they are to be invited into sales conversations. They act as a bridge that connects the different people in their network. They feed their network and become the go-to resource for their contacts. This is why modern networking is an ongoing activity, rather than a one-off deal like attending a cocktail party.

Networking requires focus, attention, and engagement, and you still have to start conversations with people you don't know. That hasn't changed. But the timeframe in which you're expecting something to happen should change. Networking leads to more sales conversations only when you don't expect something to happen immediately. Rather, you're setting yourself up for an ongoing relationship and the opportunity to leverage that relationship in the future. You really are planting seeds that you can harvest in the future.

Let's go back to the idea of meeting a potential romantic partner at a singles bar or party. As I pointed out in Chapter 8, if someone came up to you and their first question was, "Do you want to get married?" you would understandably be turned off. If they instead engage you in casual conversation and try to get to know you, many possibilities have now opened up. Maybe you will be interested in going on a date with each other. Or if not, maybe you can introduce them to a friend, or vice versa. One of the best lessons I learned about dating when I was in college came from my friend Danny. He said, "When you meet someone, even if you aren't interested in them that way, be nice, say hello, and get to know them. You never know if the woman you've been noticing all night is her best friend." He was talking about planting seeds. It works in the dating world, and it works in the business world.

This is how the Hyper-Connected salesperson gets past the gatekeepers. They position themselves as an expert in their field, a guide, and a trusted contact. They offer to serve the prospect's needs well before they ask the prospect to become a customer. Just because someone isn't ready to move forward today doesn't mean they won't be ready to move forward tomorrow. When the times comes, you want to be first in the door.

During these early networking interactions, the salesperson isn't interrupting a prospect's day and hoping for immediate action. They're simply creating a possibility for a relationship to grow when it's appropriate. If you're emailing and calling and basically using your networking as a different cold approach to new contacts, you're missing out. More and more, prospects aren't even responding to cold outreach.[50] Trying to generate business when the prospect doesn't yet know they need a product or service generates a lot of pushback. The prospect's natural defenses come into play because there isn't a track record of trust. There isn't a relationship. Even if a salesperson gets through the human and technology gatekeepers, they're still going to need to build rapport and trust if it isn't there yet.

What happens if, instead, a salesperson can approach a prospect in a non-threatening manner? Not only is the prospect much more receptive, but the salesperson now has the time to build a relationship. When the chance to move business forward later presents itself, a Hyper-Connected salesperson can leverage the social capital they've been building up over time.

Networking can be a long game, and this is why experienced salespeople in a company tend to have more access to decision-makers and therefore more success. They have simply been in the business longer, which has allowed them to create more and deeper relationships over time. Unless you have a time machine, it's impossible to short-circuit this process. The Hyper-Connected salesperson understands that planting seeds is a critical piece of the puzzle. It's not just an additive activity that's nice for when you can get around to it. Rather, it's an integral part of the prospecting and business development role.

Consistently engaging in networking activities gets the salesperson invited into a buyer's decision-making process, and it gives them much more credibility and leverage when they engage with their prospects. It can also be a much more enjoyable and constructive way of selling. It's much easier to build the "know, like, and trust" with a prospect or customer over a period of time, instead of in short interactions where you're trying to get them to act immediately. In the long run, having patience will be more rewarding for both the pocketbook and the soul.

Sales vs. Marketing

But at this point, are we still talking about selling? It sounds a lot like we're talking about marketing.

Well, we are and we aren't. In the Hyper-Connected environment, marketing and sales are going to be more intimately tied together. It doesn't really work to continue to keep them in different silos. As Charlene Li of the Altimeter Group writes, "Selling to customers in the Digital Era is difficult because, historically, almost every company divides the complex selling process among departments with specialized skills."[51] The only way to get past that is to find a way to break through the long-standing rivalry in business between the sales and marketing departments. For some reason, there's a lot of antagonism between the two functions. Maybe you haven't experienced this, but if you're selling in an organization for any period of time, you'll soon notice the little jabs that go back and forth.

As someone who has spoken to and trained many sales teams, I can attest that the easiest way to turn the room icy is to talk about the good ideas that the VP of Marketing has and why everyone should follow them. It doesn't go well. It's ironic, because sales and marketing teams are so closely aligned in their goals. Sales is more closely related to marketing than to, say, accounting.

It might be familiarity that breeds contempt. Sales teams regularly bash marketing for supplying unqualified leads, poorly informed leads, or just simply not understanding what it's like to be sitting across from the prospect, trying to get them to say yes. Conversely, marketing departments often view the sales team as a bunch of cowboys who don't respect the creativity and innovation necessary to stand out in a noisy world.

Even if this won't be changing any time soon at an institutional level, you have to change this attitude in your own mind. As Li at the Altimeter Group continued, "The difference today is that digital tools and practices are helping edge us toward a unified reality, not so much by tearing down the silos as by building windows between them. Increased visibility helps everyone in the organization operate more transparently, which makes it easier to create the seamless experiences that customers want."

In the twenty-first century, sales and marketing have never been closer. In fact, it's worth thinking of it as a spectrum, with marketing activities on one end and sales activities on the other. Different activities will fall all along the spectrum, and that's OK. In the past, a salesperson might spend all of their time on the sales side of the spectrum. Maybe she would only be making outbound calls in an attempt at a one-call close. The sales rep in this position has one job: close the sale. The only thing the rep is concerned with is picking up the phone and "dialing for dollars."

On the other end of the spectrum are activities that are purely marketing. This could be putting together a social media advertising campaign, or placing an ad in a magazine. These seem like obvious marketing tasks. But where on the spectrum is posting a status update on LinkedIn? Is that purely marketing? It would be if you were posting on a platform where you didn't know anyone, and all you wanted was an online sale. But if you're sending that post to a group of people who you have already engaged with, hoping to provide value to them, then the lines are a lot blurrier.

How about sending a birthday card, or even a birthday text, to someone who was a customer in the past? In doing this, you're creating a sales opportunity in the future, either by getting a referral or even repeat business. So it's both a marketing activity and a sales activity.

Reconciling sales and marketing isn't just a feel-good exercise; rather, it's the way to leverage the new shape of the business world. Ronald Burt is a professor at the University of Chicago's Graduate School of Business who focuses on social capital and the network structure of market profits. His book *Brokerage and Closure* is a dense collection of studies, charts, and graphs that explores how networks actually work.[52] It's not necessarily an easy read, but it's full of data showing how networks create opportunity.

> Reconciling sales and marketing isn't just a feel-good exercise; rather, it's the way to leverage the new shape of the business world.

For Burt, the data boils down to one thing: Networks create the context needed to leverage relationships. He writes, "Creativity by brokerage (networking) involves moving an idea mundane in one group to another group where the idea is new and valued." Basically, it's about taking a new idea, product, or service and bringing it to a new group. Sounds like a salesperson's job, right? Company A has a great idea for a new software program that can save Company B time and money. The salesperson connects the two.

Burt also points out that the value in the network isn't just in relationships with those who are close to us. Oftentimes, relationships with people who know the same information that we do results in little gain. However, when you're connected with people from different spheres of knowledge, there are many ways to benefit. Burt calls the gaps between different spheres of knowledge "structural holes," and these are areas of opportunity for the Hyper-Connected salesperson. By identifying the structural holes in her network and bridging them by reaching out to new groups, the Hyper-Connected salesperson carries value to new places. This is one of the main objectives of networking-based prospecting: finding and bridging these gaps in order to gain access to new spheres of influence. As Burt puts it, "People with networks rich in structural holes are the people who know about, have a hand in, and exercise control over, more rewarding opportunities."

This idea of using networking to bridge gaps between different groups of people reinforces the notion that in the Hyper-Connected landscape, networking is both a sales and marketing activity. It's about developing a web of relationships with a wide range of people. Your network should embrace variety—not just prospects and clients. When prospecting was a purely sales activity, you only wanted to network with people who would directly lead to a sale, i.e., potential clients. But these days, it makes sense to go much broader than your immediate pipeline. Effective networks have prospects, clients, referral partners, colleagues, competitors, influencers, and thought leaders. If all you're doing is connecting with prospects and customers, your network is weak. It doesn't have the depth and breadth to reliably create value.

At the same time, of course, networking should include your more immediate prospects, so it's still an important sales activity in and of itself. But by limiting your network to only those who might become customers in the short-term, you're limiting your long-term potential.

11

The Power of Brand

In the year 2015, Michael Jordan made over $110 million from his endorsements.[53] It doesn't matter that the last time he laced up a pair of basketball shoes to play in an NBA game was back in 2003. His brand has become so iconic that anybody from shoe companies to cologne manufacturers still wants to pay him. They want their customers to connect Jordan's mastery, dedication, and championship record to the company's product. Drinking Gatorade probably won't make your jump shot like Jordan's, but Gatorade sure wants you to think it will.

From the huge names like Kim Kardashian and Oprah to local celebrities like your local weatherman, companies look for individuals to attach their products and services to in an attempt to gain credibility, notoriety, or cachet. The hope is that the celebrity's emotional resonance will rub off on what they're endorsing, leading to more sales.

When we think about personal branding, many people still equate this primarily with celebrities or large companies, not everyday people. The average salesperson, while having a healthy ego, probably doesn't think they need to brand themselves as Jordan does. But brands are no longer just for ultra-famous individuals and organizations. To have success in today's Hyper-Connected world, it's critical to understand that you have a personal brand, whether you know it or not.

The Ubiquity of Your Brand

If you have a website, a social media account, or even just an email account, you're already projecting a version of yourself into the world. Your brand precedes you into your sales interactions. Your presence on digital platforms and social media creates a certain version of yourself in your prospects' minds. It plays a role in helping you start and establish relationships with the prospects and customers you want to engage with. It's important to understand that you

> Your presence on digital platforms and social media creates a certain version of yourself in your prospects' minds. It plays a role in helping you start and establish relationships with the prospects and customers you want to engage with.

can take an active role in shaping how others see you. In fact, it's critical that you do.

At its core, your personal brand is simply the perception that others have of you. It's what they think about you when you aren't around and they hear your name. When you describe someone to a colleague, the way you describe them is their brand. In the same way, the way others describe you is your brand. Personal brands have always been there, it's just that they have become more prominent in a world of social media profiles, online resumes, and dating profiles.

Ryan Rhoten, an expert in personal brand and author of *Career-Kred*, gives this example:

> If you and a few of your colleagues are talking and your boss walks in, the tone of your conversation will change, before your boss even says a word. It might stay informal if

your boss is known to be relaxed or go the other way if he's not. It might focus on certain topics and stay away from others. But there's a very real shift, and that's the boss's brand. Now flip it. And realize that when you walk into a conversation, it will shift depending on how you are perceived. That's your brand.[54]

This highlights the importance of taking an active approach to managing your personal brand. It will affect how others speak about you, and how they speak *to* you. Think about the fact that other people see only a fraction of who you are as a person. They make judgments about you based on this brief glimpse. It makes sense to control that little bit as much as possible.

Sometimes people worry that crafting a personal brand isn't genuine, that it lacks authenticity. But there's no reason to not be authentic. What we really want to do is make sure that our personal brand is representative of who we are as a person. If you're actually authentic as a person, then your brand will be authentic.

Think of your elevator speech. If it's done right, these few sentences of your introduction encapsulate how you help your customers, and who your customers are in the first place. In the same way, your personal brand should give people an easy shortcut for how to think about you and how you fit into their worldview.

Sometimes it's challenging for salespeople to understand that their prospects and clients don't actually think about them all that often. Even before the internet, it was difficult to stay on people's minds. That's only gotten harder in this high-information, low-attention world. When somebody puts their attention on us, whether it's in a conversation with a peer or in a meeting with their boss, your personal brand is going to be the shorthand way for them to think about you. And today more than ever, your prospects are relying on shorthand, because they don't have the time for anything else.

That's why we need to be deliberate and intentional with our brand. When we *do* have someone's attention, when we're in the forefront of their mind, we have to make it as easy as possible for them to understand how we fit in with their needs. You want to influence, as much as possible, where someone's thoughts go when they think about you.

In the sales world, it's actually quite easy to pinpoint what the foundation of your personal brand should be: You need people to view you as a problem-solver. That's why they're going to engage with you. When someone is thinking about your field or industry, when they're thinking about the products or services you sell, you want three thoughts to pop in their head:

1. I know someone in this field
2. They know a lot about this topic
3. I should reach out to them for help

You don't have to become a "thought leader" in your industry to build a successful brand. This is one of the biggest misconceptions about personal brand for salespeople. There's no way for everyone who sells in a particular field to become a thought leader or a widely-known expert. You don't need to be known far and wide. You just need to be seen as an expert resource by your network, by the limited group of people you're trying to influence.

Take my accountant, for example. I don't think of my accountant as a thought leader in the world of tax preparation. But he has certainly demonstrated his expertise in the past, and his monthly e-newsletter reminds me of all the different work that he can do. He's introduced me to potential clients and other professionals who are now in my sphere of influence. Does that make me more likely to continue to work with him? Yes. Am I more likely to recommend him to new business? Yes. He's not a thought leader in his industry, but from my perspective, he's an expert. You could say that he's a thought leader to me.

How Digital Communication Amplifies Your Brand

A simple way to think of this is to become a micro-influencer. You don't need to be connected to everyone. When we looked at networking in the last chapter, we saw that being a well-connected member of a network had value because it meant that you could connect people to solutions that were otherwise unknown or unavailable. It wasn't important to be known to everyone, but it was important to be known to the groups of people who you might be able to influence.

For example, if you aren't in the music industry, you probably don't know a lot of music producers, the people who oversee the recording and overall aesthetic direction of an album. They tend to work in the background. My guess is that unless you look at the liner notes or the fine-print on iTunes, you don't know who did the production on your favorite songs. But you can bet that the musicians do. And that's good, because as independent professionals who are looking for more work, producers are always selling their services. You might not know who Butch Vig or Rick Rubin is, but the people they want to sell to definitely do. They are micro-influencers in their industry. Networking and branding help them get gigs, and they're working to control the perception of their personal brand, both online and offline.

Let's look at another example, this one fictional. Even if you've never seen the television show *How I Met Your Mother*, you've probably heard of the character Barney Stinson, played by Neil Patrick Harris. An inveterate womanizer, Barney burns bridges as fast as he can build them, at least when it comes to his romantic liaisons. In one episode, an ex-girlfriend follows him around and warns everyone he meets about his past indelicacies. As a result, he makes zero headway with anyone he meets. His romantic prospects have suddenly dwindled.

This episode highlights the power of reputation in the offline world. Barney's ex-girlfriend had to literally follow people around, in person, to warn them. And once she did, they abandoned ship. The online world amplifies this and makes it easier. Imagine if Barney and ex-girlfriends could use Facebook, Instagram, or Snapchat to influence his reputation—his brand. Sure, ex-girlfriends might do their best to tarnish his brand, but Barney can still control his Facebook page, his LinkedIn profile, and other online bios to put out positive information. Barney is portrayed as an uber-successful power player in his business life, so we can imagine that he's killer at getting online recommendations and endorsements, and he would have to put a lot of work into doing so. Good or bad, one way or the other, the internet has provided multiple new pathways to amplify your personal brand. We can no longer rely on offline reputation alone, it commingles with our online presence.

The explosion of digital communication has caused personal brand to be a much more important aspect of our networking and relationship-building than ever before. In the past, we didn't have as many points of contact with our network. Branding opportunities were limited. There might have been a regular newsletter or holiday card that you would send out, but that might be about it. Most of the time, it was only possible to share your brand in person.

> We can no longer rely on offline reputation alone, it commingles with our online presence.

But now, with LinkedIn profiles, Twitter bios, and About Us pages on websites, it's much more important to consider how people view us. The combination of online and offline interactions drives how our network perceives our brand. All of these interactions can be ways of clarifying and sharing your brand:

- Your elevator speech
- Your business card
- A one-on-one coffee conversation
- Sending a physical note
- Your LinkedIn profile

- The content you share on social media sites
- Your company website
- The way you dress at a conference
- Going to a conference in the first place
- Your email newsletter
- The signature portion at the end of your emails
- Et cetera, et cetera, et cetera…

As you can see, pretty much every point of contact contains the possibility of communicating your professional brand. There are a number of great resources that can help you develop your own personal brand—check out

> **Your brand encapsulates what others think of you when you're not there.**

the websites listed at this book's online home for places to begin.

What's important is to start developing a clear conception of how you want to be known. If you haven't put much thought into this yet, you might be starting from scratch. If you have already developed the beginnings of your brand, it could be as simple as refining and clarifying what you already have. But remember, your brand encapsulates what others think of you when you're not there. Make sure that *you* have control over molding and refining this perception.

12

Balancing Short-Term Hunger with Long-Term Growth

When I was a young sales manager, I received a gift from my team. It was a plaque of the Vince Lombardi "What it Takes to be Number One" speech. They figured that since I quoted it every other week, I might as well have it on the wall.

If you've never heard or read this speech, it's the epitome of a football coach applying locker room inspiration to life in general. I loved it. It ends with a statement that perfectly connected with our sales-hustle mentality: "But I firmly believe that any man's finest hour, his greatest fulfillment to all he holds dear, is that moment when he has worked his heart out in a good cause and lies exhausted on the field of battle, victorious."[55]

From my perspective as a sales leader, being exhausted was OK, because then we would be successful. Never mind that the causal connection was never actually established—you could be exhausted without being successful. Activity, in-and-of itself, didn't necessarily cause success. At the time, I never really thought about that. My goal was to drive my salespeople, and back then, I exhorted my team to hit the phones and sell, sell, sell.

But that speech? It still gets me going, even though I like to think I've moved on from the "win or die" mentality. And in re-reading it, I realize that I missed a great line: "If you're lucky enough to find a guy with a lot of head and a lot of heart, he's never going to come off the field second."

That balance between strategy and drive perfectly describes the approach that creates success in the Hyper-Connected environment. Blind effort doesn't work anymore. The problem with comparing modern sales to football is that modern sales has layers of complexity versus the relatively simple goal of a football team. If you're a sales leader motivating a team, or

> **That balance between strategy and drive perfectly describes the approach that creates success in the Hyper-Connected environment. Blind effort doesn't work anymore.**

a producer motivating yourself, it has become necessary to think through the ideal sales activities in a way that's far more strategic than in the past.

The Union of Hunting and Farming

Earlier we looked at how my friend at CDW found top-level success by evolving his approach from a hunter mentality to a farmer mentality—by shifting focus from strenuous activity with immediate rewards (hunting) to tactical activity with long-term rewards (farming). By looking at these two approaches, we can see how both play a part in sales success. Top sales professionals in the Hyper-Connected world will continue to execute consistently on key activities, but many of those key activities have changed.

Hunting, both literally and metaphorically, is an inherently transactional process. During the literal act of hunting, you go out into the woods, seek out your prey, kill it, and eat it. All of that can happen in a matter of hours. It's short-term. It's focused on solving an immediate need: hunger. It's driven by direct, linear activity. The good thing about hunting is you can see the effects of your effort immediately. You know if you were successful right away. There's no waiting around and hoping. The bad thing about hunting is that all of your effort doesn't bleed over into the future. Once you're done eating, you have to go and do it again.

Just like real hunters might try to preserve some of their food by drying or salting it, sales hunters try to extend the benefits of the sale by building the size of the sale or asking for immediate referrals. Fundamentally, though, hunting occurs during a short window of time.

> **Top sales professionals in the Hyper-Connected world will continue to execute consistently on key activities, but many of those key activities have changed.**

Compared to hunting, farming has a long time horizon. When a farmer plants a field, it doesn't produce food immediately. It might be months before the payoff. Those intervening months require a lot of work, too. The farmer spends a lot of time watering, fertilizing, and weeding. There's a lot of cultivation that's involved. And that doesn't even include the effort needed to get the fields ready for planting, which can be substantial. If you have ever seen a postcard of the Irish countryside, you've seen the stone fences that ring all of the fields. I've been there, and really, these fences are everywhere. Sure, they look quaint now, but you have to remember that the rocks were piled up, one by one, by farmers hundreds of years ago. They were trying to clear their fields, which were unfortunately filled with rocks.

Just as a real farmer cultivates the fields, a sales farmer spends her time cultivating relationships. One of the most challenging aspects of farming, both for the actual farmer and the salesperson, is that activities rarely have a direct, noticeable impact. When you water a plant, it doesn't grow immediately. When you're engaged in a long sales cycle, every phone call isn't directly tied to a "closing" situation. This nonlinear path can be really frustrating, and it's one of the big downsides of farming.

The upside, though, is that the investment of time and effort has an amplified impact over the long term. Unlike the hunter, who has to constantly return to the forest and engage in the same activity over and over again, the farmer is creating an investment for the future. Farming scales the return that you get from your input. Even the act of preparing your farm happens only once. After that, you get to start each spring with the field already prepared. Those Irish farmers didn't have to remove the rocks from their fields over and over. Once they did it once, they were done.

> **Just as a real farmer cultivates the fields, a sales farmer spends her time cultivating relationships.**

In the sales world, proponents of the farming philosophy and the hunting philosophy sometimes butt heads. You can see the conflict play out in the current debate between the supporters of social selling and the sales leaders who focus on prospecting, prospecting, prospecting. You might have seen these arguments spill over on your favorite blog or on LinkedIn.

On the one side, the social selling advocates point to the explosion of digital communication and social media platforms. These are the new tools of the successful sales professional. We've touched on much of their research in this book. They use recent data to show that using interruption techniques such as cold calling or blast emailing don't work as well as they used to. They focus on using the new social media platforms for everything from prospecting to value-building to closing. They are the young Turks, and they sometimes deride the poor saps who keep hammering the phones like they did in the past. There's this sense that people who haven't adopted and adapted to the "New World of Selling" are unsophisticated, uneducated, or just plain dumb.

Needless to say, this doesn't go over well with many in the entrenched sales establishment. These are the people who became successful by cold calling, knocking on doors, and sending out tons of emails. They came up in the sales world where "hustle," "grit," and "activity-orientation" were put on pedestals. And the reason why? It worked. In a world of robo-callers, marketing automation, and the Do-Not-Call List, it can be easy to forget that for years, cold-calling was a completely legitimate way to start sales conversations. Even when I started my sales career 20 years ago, the phone was still an effective tool. Heck, it was one of the *only* tools.

But around that same time, it started to become harder and harder to reach people and get their attention over the phone. Salespeople and prospects were in a technology arms race. Technology made it easier to get ahold of people, but people were using the same technology to protect themselves from interruption. For example, when caller ID first came into play, that was a game-changer. Prospects loved it because they could screen calls. In response to that, new tools like *67 masked your information so that the prospect might still pick up the phone. And thus the arms race began. Sales offices would even register their business under benign names so that prospects wouldn't suspect who was on the other end of the line. Even now there is technology that makes you phone number always appear to be "local" to the person your calling.

Today, getting through to people is harder than ever, but these changes didn't appear overnight. It's been an ongoing process. And yet using the phone to reach out to customers is still the key tool for a sales hunter, regardless of its dwindling efficacy in the vast majority of industries.

It would be hard to get my 10-year-old nephew to believe that we used to pick up the phone without any idea who was on the other end. Heck, these days it's hard to get people to pick up even when they *do* know who's calling. Our phones are now used just as often for texting and email. According to a Gallup Poll conducted in 2014, 68% of 18-29-year-olds had texted the day before, compared to only 50% who had used the phone for calling. And even with those between the ages of 30 and 49, 47% had texted versus only 41% who had spoken on a call.[56]

Just making calls isn't going to cut it anymore. Cold emails have lost most of their effectiveness as well. Spam filters, junk boxes, and the squeezed attention span of the average professional makes it hard to get noticed. In an environment where people regularly get 100, 200, or 300+ emails in a day, do you really expect your cold emails to be effective? Remember, there were 2.5 million emails sent *every second* as of early 2017.[57] If you started in sales 30 years ago, you might think cold approaches will still work. That's because they did work back then. But in a world where attention is at a premium, interjecting yourself into your prospect's day isn't going to be efficient.

These cold approaches aren't dead, but they can't remain the cornerstone of your sales activities. In a study done in 2014, the Keller Center for Research at Baylor University reported on the effectiveness of cold calling for real estate agents.[58] They tracked 6,264 cold calls to see how effective they were at generating business. The results? "Collectively, we see that it will take an investment of approximately 7.5 hours to complete 209 calls, leading to a return of one appointment or referral." That's not super-efficient, but those are still results.

> **There's still a need for drive and consistent activity in a Hyper-Connected environment, and we can still focus on and track this activity.**

So let's be really clear about the future. It's not that cold calling is dead. It's that it's less efficient and more frustrating. Would you like to make 209 phone calls to get one appointment? Instead of holding on to cold calling, we can instead hold to the work ethic that cold calling entails. As we saw in Chapter 9, there's still a need for drive and consistent activity in a Hyper-Connected environment, and we can still focus on and track this activity.

When you examine the hunting paradigm, that's really what the cold calling champions are focused on: activity that can be tracked, analyzed, and improved. We can integrate this into Hyper-Connected selling. It's easy to see a clear connection between the farmer mentality and being successful in a Hyper-Connected world. But it would be a mistake to think that it's only about being a farmer.

> There's a false dichotomy that's been built up between the cold calling camp and social selling camp. Instead, I want you to think of it as a spectrum. Success is found somewhere in the middle.

Too often, this metaphor is used as though hunting and farming are mutually exclusive—you have to do one or the other. There's a false dichotomy that's been built up between the cold calling camp and social selling camp. Instead, I want you to think of it as a spectrum. Success is found somewhere in the middle.

In the sales world, there's no such thing as a one-size-fits-all balance between hunting and farming. The ideal mix of short- and long-term sales activities will vary depending on your goals, where you're at in your career, your industry, and even your personality. Your aim should be to find a balance between activities that

> Success in the Hyper-Connected world comes from pulling activities from both sides. It comes from being both a farmer and a hunter.

get you direct results, reaping the benefits of seeds you've planted in the past, and investing in relationships that will create benefits in the future.

In Buddhism, there's something called the "Middle Path," which is all about avoiding the extremes. We can take something from that philosophy. Think about walking the middle path when building your sales networks. It's not about being on social media sites all day, constantly pinging your network in an attempt to get sales. It's not about pounding the phone day after day, either. Success in the Hyper-Connected world comes from pulling activities from both sides. It comes from being both a farmer and a hunter.

Balancing Short-Term and Long-Term Activity

When working to build our relationships, we have to remember the end goal: identifying and engaging with potential clients. Relationships for the sake of relationships isn't what we're going after. Posting on social media just to say we did it ends up being a waste time.

The goal is to create a balance of sales activities. If all you did last week was engage in long-term relationship building, you probably had a hard time hitting your sales goals. And if you muscle through each day on sales calls or endless emails and messages, you'll burn out. Imagine a teeter-totter (also known as a seesaw, depending on where you live!) with long-term relationship-building activities on one end, and your direct prospecting and sales activities on the other. If you put too much weight on either side, it won't move at all. Your process gets stuck. If, however, you create a balance on both sides, you'll create flow. It's not "either-or" in the Hyper-Connected world. It's "both-and."

So what does it look like on the ground when a salesperson brings these tools together? For one, we can take the old paradigm's focus on activity and shift it to engaging with both our online contacts and offline network. Imagine if every sales rep on a team spends one hour a day using social media platforms to read their newsfeeds, interact with a set number of contacts, and curate and post a certain amount of content. When engaging in these activities, it's important to be intentional. It's too easy for online activity to devolve into just random surfing. Here's where the old-school skills come in handy. Getting off track is a long-standing issue for salespeople, which is why sales teams have tracked metrics for years. It's just that now we're tracking new categories.

Social selling leaders advocate taking the cold calls of the past and making them warm calls. Whenever possible, social media and digital communications can be used to get inside the gates. This way, we don't have to waste time and energy trying to bash them down. In many contexts, there's no need to start from scratch with a name and no information on the prospect. There are so many ways for us to research and engage that weren't available before. Now, instead of having just a checklist involving a goal-number for cold calls made each day, we can also create checklists that track a set number of social selling activities every day. And we can still track the number of warm leads by phone or email, and how many led to success.

In addition to spending an hour per day on social media, today's sales team might spend an hour or two researching potential clients using online tools to explore their prospects' needs: what's going on in the industry, what prospects are posting about on social media, what content they're sharing. Sales teams might also research what's happening both professionally and personally for the people they want to start or build relationships with. Honestly, it's amazing what people share when you start paying attention to their Twitter feeds. Research from the IDC shows that up to 75% of buyers use social media and digital tools during their research phase.[59] Doesn't it make sense to spend time in the same waters as your prospects?

The old-school, mechanistic approach to selling had a fine appreciation for tracking and metrics, and we can keep that. We *should* keep that. We don't have to throw the baby out with the bath water. At the same time, though, we need to accept more ambiguity and fuzziness, because today's metrics aren't always as clear-cut as "number of calls/number talked to/number of appointments set." That's no longer the nature of the world we live in. We should stop trying to pound round pegs into square holes. Whether you're managing yourself or a sales manager leading others, it's important to keep the focus on long-term goals while understanding that the shortest distance to them might not be a straight line.

Think of what a sales meeting looks like for a Hyper-Connected sales team. Can you imagine Alec Baldwin's sales manager character from *Glengarry Glen Ross* berating his team for not posting enough on LinkedIn? Would he still tell them that coffee is for closers? Probably not. Instead, he might say that coffee is for those who build long-term, mutually beneficial relationships with key influencers and contacts in the industry.

It's not about brute force anymore, but you can still look at metrics that combine the short-term with the long-term. These metrics might include:

- # of LinkedIn status updates posted per week
- # of LinkedIn status updates liked or commented upon per week
- # of tweets and retweets per week
- # of in-person networking opportunities attended
- # of in-person or phone 1:1 "coffee meetings" set with networking partners
- # of introductions made
- # of industry articles read and shared
- # of relationships moved forward
- # of calls
- # of sales appointments/demos performed
- # of sales "asks"

As your career evolves, you can change how much emphasis you give each activity. For example, if you're new in your industry or your career, it makes sense to search for immediate opportunities. You have to hit your quota or sales goals. This could mean calling inbound leads, attending networking events and conferences with the goal of meeting people, and trying to convert every opportunity you get your hands on. You haven't had a chance to plant seeds in the past that you can harvest for success in the present. It's going to require some effort as you muscle through the beginning of your career. At the same time, though, you need to be finding investment opportunities that will pay off in the future. Even if it's just a percentage of your time every day, say 10-20%, it's important to invest in relationships that will have benefits down the road. This could be spending time on your online presence, identifying and building stronger relationships with key centers of influence in your industry, or studying to become an expert in your field.

As you create a larger network and deepen the relationships you have, you will start to invest more time in your long-term activities. If you've been in your field for a couple of decades, much more of your time will be spent on relationship-building and relationship-maintaining activities. Successful sales veterans use cold approaches less frequently because they have such a rich pool of resources to tap into. Of course, veteran salespeople still have all of the same approaches available to them that a newbie does, and sometimes they still need to use them. But they're also able to leverage their past investments to get referrals and introductions.

Do a quick analysis of your business. Where are you right now? Are you spending more time on hunting or farming activities? There isn't a "right" answer, but you should be aware of how you're spending your time. Pay attention to which of your activities have long-term payoffs, and which don't. Like a farmer, you want to plant and cultivate as many seeds as you can. You'll hunt in the short term to make sure you can still eat (hit your sales numbers). But don't lose sight of the long-term vision: Creating relationships and opportunities that you will continuously harvest in a way that's easier, more efficient, and more effective than going hunting every day.

13

Harnessing Social Technology

B y this point in the book, you might be overwhelmed by two impulses:

1. I need to get my arms around the changes in the sales world! I want to be on the leading edge, not the trailing edge.
2. How the hell will I do that while still dealing with the daily activities of selling?!

This isn't a bad place to be. You should be asking yourself which tools, tactics, and skills are needed to change the way you sell, but you should do it wisely and efficiently. It's an exciting time in sales, because you have more tools available now than ever before. Our goal for the remainder of the book is to look at how we can use the tools available in the Hyper-Connected world to start, strengthen, and leverage connections with our networks.

Dynamic vs. Passive Uses of the Internet

The internet has been the main driver of change in the sales world, and online tools are also the biggest opportunity for sales professionals. It has become impossible for the sales profession to ignore the online world. In 2016, there were 3.8 million Google searches conducted every minute.[60] All of those searches led to a website—maybe your own company's website, or one of your social media profiles. InternetLiveStats.com reported that by March 2016, the number of live websites had surpassed and stayed above 1 billion.[61] On one of them, Facebook, 3.3 million posts are added every minute. On another, YouTube, 500 hours of video are uploaded every minute. The digital world is a very big, and very busy, place.

Is there room in this busy, bustling, noisy place for the average sales rep? Absolutely. The internet abounds with opportunity. We just need to know where to look. We have seen over the course of this book how a buyer's experience has changed substantially, and why this necessitates a corresponding change in the seller's experience. Now that we have established the importance of starting, building, and leveraging our sales relationships differently, we can look at how to use the new online tools in service of these objectives.

This is why, in a book entitled *Hyper-Connected Selling*, we're looking at technology last, not first. How we use technology, especially digital communication and social media platforms, should be driven by our business goals, and not the other way around. As salespeople, our business goal is to engage with our prospects, customers, and networks in a way that provides value for them, and access and credibility for us. We need to link digital tools with accomplishing those goals. We need to figure out how these tools can help us, rather than being deep, dark wells that we fall into and waste time in. And many of us know all too well how easy it is to waste time on the internet.

Luckily for us, there are many ways to do it right.

Let's begin by thinking about how we want to "show up" online. Whether you're a brand-new salesperson fresh out of school or a 40-year veteran, you have to think about how you will represent yourself through digital media. As we saw in Chapter 11, our online reputations precede us. The digital world takes our personal brand and shares it far and wide. It's a force multiplier that provides exponential growth in how we share our message. It's imperative that we get crystal clear about what that brand is, because our brand is out there. People are judging us on it, whether we want them to or not.

Ryan Rhoten, a digital business coach, calls this living in a "digital forward world."[62] It's as though a portfolio of our careers gets sent ahead of us to anyone who interacts with us, or who is even considering interacting with us. And there's no hiding from it. Even sales reps with a very limited online presence are subject to this, because in today's sales world, the absence of a LinkedIn profile or something similar speaks for itself in ways you might not realize. It also points to how you can leverage your message to help fulfill your goals.

This makes me think of the movie *A Knight's Tale,* which had Mark Addy playing a fictional Chaucer. He was the hype man who announced the knight of the movie's title, played by Heath Ledger, before each bout. Addy's character would tell the captive audience about all of his liege's exploits. After this enthusiastic introduction, every opponent knew what to expect when the knight came onto the field. This reminds me, too, of the Daenerys Targaryen character on *Game of Thrones*. Her entrance is preceded by such a dizzying array of descriptors—Mother of Dragons, the Unburnt, Queen of the Andals, Khaleesi of the Great Grass Sea, Breaker of Chains— that frankly, at this point it's difficult to keep track.

Now imagine you had one of those medieval criers going into every sales meeting ahead of you. Well, you sort of do, because that's what your online presence does for you. It shares that story 24/7 with no effort on your part, and whether you want it to be happening or not. From big gorillas like Facebook or LinkedIn to niche sites serving specific industries, you can make a lot of choices about how you spend your time online. All of your efforts on these sites can be divided into two types: dynamic and passive.

Dynamic activities require us to be actively engaged on the sites. Many of the activities that are usually associated in our minds with social media fall into this category. They require you to be online, engaging with others through these platforms. This includes sending out status updates on Facebook, commenting on LinkedIn posts, and liking a Tweet. These are all proactive uses of digital communication. So is sending out e-newsletter blasts, using your CRM for marketing automation, or even texting your prospects. Whether it's reaching out directly to a prospect, influencing your network by sharing content, or researching your clients, these activities are designed to actively further your possible sales engagements.

These dynamic activities are very powerful, but they can also be overwhelming and lead to wasted time. There's always another conversation you can join, or a new post you could engage with. Social media sites are never-ending rivers of content. It's easy to get bogged down by online interactions or waste time in superficial chatter. These dynamic activities are important, but it's imperative to control how you're engaging. The key is to be intentional with your time. What you do and how you do it is your choice. Sometimes you need to step back from the process and make sure that your activities are in alignment with your goals.

> These dynamic activities are important, but it's imperative to control how you're engaging.

One of the biggest challenges for sales reps right now is that they feel beholden to technology. If you don't feel like you're in control, it's time to take the power back. In the book *Mindful Tech,* Stanford technologist David Levy examined the role that technology plays in our lives,[63] writing about how mindfulness exercises can help people control their online behaviors. He wrote, "they come to see how they've allowed their online activities to be governed by unexamined rules and expectations, as well as unconscious habits. And they realize that they actually have much greater choice in the matter." Levy points out that just because an email shows up in your inbox, or there's a conversation happening on Facebook, it doesn't mean you have to jump and respond. You get to choose.

It's easy to feel that we're at the beck and call of our network. Most of us have smartphones or laptops with us wherever we go. When you're ultra-responsive, though, you aren't as effective with your time. You're always being reactive, not proactive. You're being controlled by the technology.

Don't lose sight of the fact that digital communication is optional. That's right, you don't have to do it. It's just a tool. Saying that you must actively engage online is like saying that you must use email to be successful. You actually don't. Of course, using email makes life a whole lot easier and more effective. But if you have a ridiculously morbid fear of Gmail, you could figure out other ways of communicating with people, and it's the same thing with social media. I've spent a decade showing people how to use LinkedIn for sales, but I've never once claimed that you have to post on LinkedIn to be successful, because it isn't true. Yes, it can do a lot to support your goals, and not participating can mean that you're losing out on opportunities. But there are still ways to be successful without using these various methods.

Now for the big "but."

It's true that active uses of social media, texting, and online communication are your choice. But if you're choosing to pass them up, you'd better be making up for it somewhere else, because these are important, effective tools. And when we start thinking about the *passive* online tools available to a salesperson, you don't have as much of a choice.

Passive activities are online activities that don't require ongoing engagement. These passive uses of online tools might include:

- Creating and maintaining a website
- Your LinkedIn Profile
- Establishing a Facebook page for your business
- Other online bios and profiles, such as on Twitter
- Managing what shows up in a Google search for your name

These are considered passive not because they don't require effort, but because they're available for your network to consume on their terms. It requires some work up front, but then it exists on the internet, and your audience can engage with it on their own schedule. This is material you make available for anyone to discover and digest.

The impact this content has, though, is anything but passive. Think of buyers who are looking for information and guidance as they begin their journey. The first place they engage with you is through the passive content you've created online. Think of digital passive activity as being like the Ronco Rotisserie Oven they sell on infomercials late at night. The goal is to "set it and forget it" so that the best information is available to your network whenever they need it.

> I'd argue that salespeople can skimp on dynamic activities (so long as they're making up for it somewhere else), but can no longer ignore these passive uses of social media and other digital platforms.

I'd argue that salespeople can skimp on dynamic activities (so long as they're making up for it somewhere else), but can no longer ignore these passive uses of social media and other digital platforms. Remember that these passive uses *aren't about you*. They are about your prospects, your clients, and your network in general. When prospects are looking for information and they can't find it, this gums up the works. Whether they want to vet you, get connected with information about your company or your field, or even just find your contact data, if they can't find that information, you have a black mark.

Would you want to work with a company that doesn't have a website? You might question whether they're a real entity. It's the same with your personal online presence. Your prospects and customers want to be able to look you up. If they can't find any information on you, it's going to destroy your credibility. We live in a world where potential customers expect you or your company to have a website, and that's just the way it is. If you're good at what you do, or if you're an expert in your field, you do your prospects a major disservice by being hard to find.

For example, let's say you don't feel like spending time on your LinkedIn profile today, or even this month or this year. But the prospects you're meeting with at 11:30 want to get information about you beforehand, and they look you up. If they do a quick Google search and can't find anything, or find a barebones presence, they won't be as excited about the meeting. They see an incomplete profile and are left to make their decisions about you on their own, without any input or guidance from you.

The person looking up your information doesn't see the 3-D person that you really are. They have to make their decisions based on whatever they can find about you. You have depth, nuance, experience, perspective, and personality in the offline world. But all they have is the social media profiles and websites that they find with an online search. And that really goes to the heart of why it's important to manage your brand online.

Letting Your Online Profiles Speak for You

In the Hyper-Connected world, your prospects will make decisions about you before they even reach out. They're deciding if you have the knowledge and expertise to be their Sales Sherpa. Our digital presence precedes us, and we have to share information in a way that helps prospects make the decision to engage. Think about this: Digital natives will continue to move into decision-making positions. Over the next few years, they will become your buyers, and they will take their online proficiency with them into the vetting process.

Even today, research shows that 85% of Millennial decision-makers use social media to research products and services for their companies.[64] It used to be that we extended trust to each other provisionally when we first met, and then built a relationship on top of that by sharing information to justify that initial trust. That's been flipped on its head. Now we can vet people before deciding to give them any of our time or bothering to build a relationship.

Let's go back to the dating world analogy. Before technology implanted itself into the dating process, it was hit or miss. The only ways to meet people were at social gatherings, in those singles bars we mentioned earlier, or maybe through a referral from a friend. You would meet someone, decide whether there was mutual attraction and interest, then perhaps decide to go on a more formal date. And on that date and each subsequent one, you would decide whether or not to continue to build the trust and the relationship based on what you found out about each other along the way.

Enter online dating. I might not have to tell you much about it, because there's a good chance that you've tried it. A Pew Research study showed that 22% of 18- to 24-year-olds had used a mobile dating app in 2015. We're not even talking about websites, just an app.[65] According to Match.com, over 40 million Americans have tried online dating at some point.[66]

As we know, online dating flips the traditional trust-building process on its head. Instead of knowing almost nothing about a person before the first date, now we have full profiles telling us about their interests, background, and attitudes. And they also have all of that information about you! The decision about who to spend an hour over coffee with is now much more informed.

As professionals, of course, we don't live completely in the online world. So how does our digital presence impact our real-world engagements? We can stay in the dating world for another scenario showing the bridge between the online and offline world. It's one I know well, because it's the story of when I first started dating my wife.

My wife and I met while salsa dancing. That sounds pretty old-school, right? She gave me her phone number, but because of conflicting schedules, it was almost a month before our first date, and during that month we exchanged over 100 text messages. That might not seem like a lot for a high school kid, but for adults, that's quite a bit. On our third date, she started our conversation by saying, "I read your blog." She had actually done a Google search on me, and because I was active online, she found my LinkedIn profile, my Twitter account, and my blog. She knew a lot about me as a person based on those platforms—and luckily, she kept going out with me.

This scenario has become familiar in the offline world, and it's why it's so important to manage your brand online. Your online presence *will* follow you into the offline world.

In many ways, "passive" activity is a misnomer, because you certainly aren't passive in its creation or curation. You want to be very diligent and focused on putting your best foot forward online. You never know when someone is going to engage with that material. It could be a brand new prospect or a networking partner. It could also be a decision-maker coming in later in the process, needing to be brought up to speed. If they don't know the salesperson involved, that information should be just a quick online search away.

> In many ways, "passive" activity is a misnomer, because you certainly aren't passive in its creation or curation.

Do a quick Google search of yourself. Put your name plus your company, or your name plus your city, and see what comes up. This isn't a vain, self-centered exercise. It's valuable research. What comes up when you Google your name is what comes up when someone else searches for you. You have to decide whether it's what you want people to know about you.

Going back to the conversation we had about branding in Chapter 11, think about whether your brand comes through in that Google search. Can a visitor who knows little about you, what you sell, or your company quickly ascertain your main areas of focus?

Can they figure out what you do immediately, or would they have to dig? If it's not readily apparent, you have a problem. In a world of attention overwhelm, prospects aren't going to give you much time or bandwidth. You have to make it easy for them.

The Google search gives you a starting point for harnessing your online brand. This is when it makes sense to think like a marketer. If someone's first experience of you is the results from that Google search, would it tell the story that you want to tell? Consider this from the perspective of the searcher. They know absolutely nothing about you, and then they're presented with whatever information pops up. You need to make sure the information is updated, accurate, clear, and specific. The more clarity you've brought to your message, the easier it is to share. Create a niche that you focus on. It makes it much easier to share your message and shape how others view you. The more focused you are, the easier it is for someone to grasp what you do.

It's easy to go down a rabbit hole and spend hours and hours poring over the results of Google searches and how they change over time, so be smart about it. Remember that this is brand research, not random surfing. There's no need to panic and revamp your entire strategy from scratch without forethought, or spend days on LinkedIn hoping to move your profile up on Google. Every hour spent working on your LinkedIn profile is an hour that you weren't engaging with prospects and clients. So don't go overboard, but do be strategic.

Most Google searchers won't go past the first page of results.[67] What you want to do is make sure that you get the right information on the first websites that show up. And if there's something that isn't helping you, make sure that you work to have that result drop lower.

Your goal is to create a self-referential ecosystem of information about you and your company online. It sounds technical, but it's actually quite simple. You want to ensure that there are a number of sites that accurately and clearly spell out the value you bring to your prospects and clients. You want to ensure that all of these sites are linked to one another and repeat your message. This way, a viewer who finds one site can easily go to other platforms where you're reinforcing your message. These online points of message amplification might include:

> **Your goal is to create a self-referential eco-system of information about you and your company online.**

- Your LinkedIn profile
- Your company's website
- Your company's LinkedIn page
- Your Twitter bio
- An Instagram or Pinterest page
- An online bio
- A bio on your school's alumni registry
- An online industry association article about you
- A podcast that features you being interviewed
- A blog article about you and your company

While it's easy to bemoan the work and time necessary to create a solid online presence, remember how powerful this is. Twenty years ago, salespeople would have loved a way to share information about themselves and their company in a format that was easy to access 24 hours a day, 7 days a week. And now we have it.

Approach this as a value-adding opportunity rather than a pain in the rear. Social media profiles are the first place that people think of when they consider their online brand, and for good reason. People are looking each other up. A lot. LinkedIn itself is the third most-used search engine online. According to author Jeff Bullas, there are over a billion searches done on LinkedIn every day, which puts it right after Google and YouTube.[68] Facebook, while more on the personal than professional side, has over a billion daily users. That's a billion. A day. It makes sense to harness your profiles on these sites, because a few of these users just might be stopping by to check you out. If you don't take the time to craft your presence on these sites, you're abandoning important touch points with your network. You might not visit these sites all the time, but your contacts do.

There are many resources out there to walk you through the basics of creating optimized online profiles. An easy way to approach the process is to think of it as a sales call. If you're about to meet someone who doesn't know you on a sales call, what would you share about yourself? That's the same material that belongs in your profile.

As a corollary to that, remember to not be completely self-centered. Don't stop at listing your sales awards and telling your visitors how ama- zeballs you are. That's like meeting someone new and having your eleva-

> **As much as possible, share in a way that would be of interest to your reader.**

tor pitch be filled with self-praise and chest puffing. They're on your online profile because they want to find out if you can help them solve whatever problem they're working on, not because they couldn't find your autobiography on Amazon. As much as possible, share in a way that would be of interest to your reader.

The noted rhetoric (i.e. persuasion) professor Michael Drout once said, "Good rhetoric isn't about what you want to say, it's about what they need to hear. So share what they need to hear."[69] This wise sentiment couldn't be more relevant.

While you can control your own personal profiles, you might not have as much control over your company's digital presence. It will be important to create an alignment between what your company's website is saying at an organizational level and what your profile says on a personal level. If someone reads all of these at the same time, they should have a coherent message about how you serve your end clients. That doesn't mean you should be cutting and pasting from your company website to your LinkedIn profile, though. That's too obvious to your reader and actually breaks down the trust you're trying to build. Instead, look for themes, phrases, and important ideas that permeate your company's web presence, and look to bring those into your profile.

When you put all of these pieces together, you'll have an online presence that clearly and accurately tells your story. It's a powerful way to position yourself as a micro-influencer and a Sales Sherpa. If this is the extent of your activity online, you're going to be well-poised to take advantage of the Hyper-Connected world. You will have given yourself an opportunity to engage with your prospects, clients, partners, and anyone else who wants to find out more about you.

You could stop here, but I don't necessarily advise it. As I've mentioned, the most important online activities are the passive ones. At the very least, you need to have some sort of online presence so that prospects can find you when they're looking. But once you've established your online presence, there's a whole lot you can do with it. Let's now turn to examining how your online activities can be used to continuously leverage and expand your network.

14

Playing the Digital Numbers Game Wisely

At one point in my career, I went in for an interview with a company that was hiring sales reps for their multi-use, space-age paper media duplication and transmission platform. In other words, I would be selling copier machines. They had been coy on the phone, but in the interview I realized what their prospecting process was: I would be assigned a few city blocks in downtown Chicago full of high-rise office buildings. I would start at the top floor of each building and work my way down, knocking at each office. When I got to the bottom, I'd go to the building across the street and start the process over.

This used to be a common approach for salespeople trying to canvass a territory. I was reminded of the old-school door-to-door book sales reps who were dropped off on the corner in the morning and given an address miles away where they'd be picked up that evening. Or the B2B salespeople who would go to office parks, writing down the names of all the companies on the mailboxes, then calling on each one. The nice thing about this sales style was the reps knew the general shape and size of what they were working with, and they knew who they would be interacting with. If they were selling photocopiers, they could look at the building directory and know that their goal was to get in front of the decision-makers from AAA Mortgages all the way to Zany Entertainment Productions.

The physical limitations of the past are no longer an issue. It's possible to be based in North Carolina and have customers from Maine to San Diego, or from Manitoba to Shanghai. I recently had a friend move from Chicago back to Madison, Wisconsin to be near his family. There wasn't even a hiccup in his business. He works nationally, and many of his customers are only a call, email, or video chat away. Ironically, this wide-open vista can hamper our reach as easily as it can create it. Digital communication has opened up so many opportunities, but it has caused many salespeople to freeze up or get overwhelmed. It's like looking at a tall mountain and trying to figure out how to climb it—it can be easier to worry about the challenge than actually beginning to tackle it. In the Hyper-Connected world, it's important to scale your digital work and forge an easier pathway up that mountain.

> **In the Hyper-Connected world, it's important to scale your digital work and forge an easier pathway up that mountain.**

Creating Your Own Digital Neighborhood

Most of this book has focused on the opportunities of digital communication and networking. But there's a downside to all of this: it's hard to know where to start. Most of us don't like going to parties where we don't know anyone. Well, how about showing up at a party with millions of people you don't know? When the number of active users on Facebook, YouTube, Google Plus, Instagram, and Twitter are compared to the populations of countries, they'd each be in the top 10 worldwide.[70] And those are just the large networks that are focused in North America. If your business has a global scope, there are the large networks that span Europe, Asia, India, and Latin America like Qzone, Sina, Weibo, and Xing.

These numbers, and the possibilities that come with them, have blown up the old ideas of a sales network. Some sellers see these numbers as a vista full of opportunity. They chase numbers of connections and contacts like they're trying to win a prize. You have users on LinkedIn, for example, called L.I.O.Ns (LinkedIn Open Networkers) who brag about the number of people in their network: 5,000; 10,000; 30,000. But this type of strategy usually isn't the best one.

In a Hyper-Connected world, connectivity is just the beginning. In most ways, being connected is less valuable than ever because it's so much easier to connect. Connecting with someone online doesn't always mean they're now in your sphere of influence. It's a place to start, but there's still a lot of continued contact and trust-building that needs to happen before you would call them a prospect.

> It's like saying everyone is a prospect just because you have a phone book. That ignores all of the work that actually goes into the prospecting and qualifying process.

It's like saying everyone is a prospect just because you have a phone book. That ignores all of the work that actually goes into the prospecting and qualifying process. Connecting digitally still requires slogging through a lot of unqualified people before you find the valuable ones. Just because much of the world is now an email or Facebook message away, it doesn't mean that the entire world is now in your prospect pipeline. Starting a conversation with "Hi, we're connected on LinkedIn!" or "I saw that we have similar Twitter followers" doesn't have much impact. So how can a salesperson make these large numbers work for them instead of against them?

Before we dive in, first consider what your connection strategy is. In the past, it wasn't as necessary to think about your network strategically because you mostly connected with people you physically came into contact with. So your network strategy was largely defined by your geographical location. But now, you can jump on any number of sites for hours and connect with people anywhere. That's incredibly powerful, but with that power comes a price: it's easy to get wrapped up in connecting with people just because you can.

As we discussed in Chapter 13, we must always go back to connecting our digital activity with our business goals. The purpose of our sales network is to help drive sales opportunities. If you lose sight of your purpose, you'll have a lot of connections and very few prospects. Spamming hundreds of people on LinkedIn to connect doesn't necessarily get you closer to your goals. As one of my early mentors told me, "Don't confuse activity and action. Just because you're doing something doesn't mean you are actually *doing* something."

> **If you're going to be a micro-influencer, you'll want to develop a sphere of influence that doesn't try to incorporate everyone.**

It's easy to think that because we're theoretically connected to everyone on the internet, we should be bringing a huge chunk of people into our sphere of influence. It's important to resist this impulse. If you're really focused on serving a specific segment of the market, it makes sense to be tied more closely to that segment. If you're going to be a micro-influencer, you'll want to develop a sphere of influence that doesn't try to incorporate everyone. You want to have relevance for the people in your network and vice versa.

You want to find a balance point between the reach that online communication gives you and developing trust with the people you're connecting with. Sociologist Mark Granovetter authored *The Strength of Weak Ties* in 1973, a paper that became one of the most-cited in his field. It examined how people used social connections to find new work,[71] and his research showed that most people found new jobs through people they knew, i.e. their networks. That probably doesn't surprise you, but the type of relationship that drove many of these referrals might: Most people found new jobs not through people they knew very well, but through what was called a *weak tie*. At the time, this was defined as people you saw less than once a week, but more than once a year. It's amazing to see how much our conception of what constitutes a "weak tie" has changed since 1973.

Granovetter's research showed that the power of the network wasn't built on the closeness of the connections, but rather upon having access to different spheres of influence and information. The person you see every day has access to the same knowledge that you do, which isn't always helpful. The person you run into at an industry conference once a year comes to the relationship with a host of new information that can lead to new opportunities.

You don't need to be best friends with someone to leverage the relationship for business purposes. Think back to Ronald Burt's research on how networks provide value, which we discussed in Chapter 10. It's important to act as a connector between two different spheres of knowledge or groups

> **Salespeople act as the bridge between their company and the various spheres of influence of their prospects.**

of people. Salespeople act as the bridge between their company and the various spheres of influence of their prospects. So when I talk about being a micro-influencer in your field, be sure not to define your field too narrowly. It's all about finding the balance of casting a wide net, but only in precisely-defined parts of the ocean.

In order to influence the right people, you need to have both access and trust. This is why you need that balance. Access without trust doesn't get you there. Online platforms allow you to extend your reach and create relationship-building opportunities with a relatively small amount of effort. However, reaching out and connecting to someone isn't enough to start a sales conversation. If you approach networking online as a mad dash for numbers, that's the same as passing out and collecting business cards willy-nilly in the old days. Just because you have someone's email address or Twitter handle doesn't mean that you've established the foundation of a relationship.

The key word we're looking at is balance. If you only connect with people you already know well, you aren't giving yourself the opportunity to cultivate more weak relationships. But if you instead reach out blindly, you end up with a large number of contacts who are hard to manage and hard to leverage. You're going to have to feel out what the perfect place is for you. This balance isn't a static concept, it's a dynamic one. It's natural for your network to expand and contract over time as you build, develop, and refine your sales network.

I once did an interview with Will Barron of *The Salesman Podcast*, and I looked at what a new salesperson just starting out in a sales career should do to build their network.[72] I pointed out that when someone is relatively new to the workforce, it's important for them to focus on actually growing the size of their network. Their activities should be focused on adding to the people they know. In contrast, someone who has been in their field for twenty years will take a much different approach. They have already spent their career building relationships, and it's more important for them to manage and refine those relationships.

It's also important to remember that not every digital connection is created equal. Each social media site and app has a different culture and ethos for proper usage, and every industry has a different set of standards and etiquette for professional interaction. Even beyond that, while you don't want to get trapped by stereotypes, it's important to consider the field you work in and what kind of personalities tend to be attracted to it. If you're selling to financial service professionals, there will probably be different expectations for online behavior than if you sell to graphic designers, computer programmers, or heavy manufacturers.

If you're at the very beginning phase of establishing an online presence, oftentimes the best place to start is with your offline contacts. LinkedIn is a good place for young professionals because it has relatively high penetration and so many people are on it. Focus on connecting to your existing colleagues, clients, and partners. From there, you have access to information that you didn't have before, such as who these initial connections are connected with. That can give you a quick boost to prospecting, and these numbers tend to uptick exponentially—I just checked my LinkedIn account, and I now have over 2 million second-level connections. LinkedIn's early (and lasting) appeal has been the ability to see who your connections are connected to. Even before they developed Sales Navigator, savvy salespeople were using LinkedIn to create warm introductions to their sales leads.

But how many sales relationships can the average salesperson even manage? Ten? Twenty? One hundred? One thousand? We actually have a pretty good idea of how many relationships a human being can manage from

> **Technology has always been there to help us manage new capabilities.**

research done by anthropologist Robin Dunbar. Now known as Dunbar's Number, the number of relationships an average person can manage, at the level of being somewhat involved in the relationship, is 148. That's really not that many. And even if you suppose salespeople are wired to be better at relationships (which is a stretch at best) and can manage twice the average, that's only three hundred relationships. If sales reps want to wrap their heads around networks and prospect lists that number into the thousands, they aren't going to do it on their own.

Technology has always been there to help us manage new capabilities. It helps us scale our efforts to deal with the new opportunities and challenges. When telephones came around, we didn't develop the ability to remember the phone number of everyone we knew—we just wrote them down in a phone book. Same thing with our physical and email addresses. And we don't need to remember who was in a movie any more, or the air-speed velocity of an unladen swallow, because we can just look it up with IMDB or Google.

Trying to manage our large networks without technology would be futile, but with social media, we can continue to build and create networks by outsourcing a lot of the work to the technology. We won't become best friends with everyone in our online networks, and we don't have to. But the existence of the connections gives us a chance to maintain and develop the relationships that we might actually be able to leverage down the road.

Online Interaction as a Force Multiplier

Let's say you've already put the time and effort into honing your online presence. You've considered your overall sales strategy and how digital communication fits. You've crafted your online profiles to share the messages that you want. Your LinkedIn profile has been optimized, your Twitter bio has been crafted, and you have a bio on your company's webpage. You've reached out and connected with your existing network on the main social media sites. You are ready to rock.

So now what?

I started teaching people how to use LinkedIn for business in 2008, soon after it hit the internet. One question that comes up over and over again is, "What do I actually do with this?" Variations of the question include: "How do I engage with my network on social media? How does this get me more business?"

In the past few chapters, we looked at creating an online presence that will share your message with anyone who is looking for it. Whether these are new networking partners, prospects you've recently reached out to, or a client you've been working with for years, they can find and engage with your information online.

Unfortunately, that's not enough to truly excel in the Hyper-Connected world. To borrow a term from poker, those are table stakes. You need those in place just to play the game. But if you want to *win* the game, it becomes more important to actively engage online. These are the active, dynamic tools of digital communication that we looked at in the last chapter: Not simply establishing your online accounts and websites, but using them frequently and actively enough to expand or leverage your network.

When it comes to the dynamic uses of digital communication, the rules become a bit less clear. It's not because they're less important, but because the pathways to success are so much more variable. As the social selling evangelist Jack Kosakowski points out, "There isn't a clear set of best practices that works for every salesperson in every industry in every situation. You can't apply blanket rules to everybody."[73]

In the future, it seems likely that activity in the online world will become the main lever that allows us to move forward through our sales processes. Because this process is non-linear, it can be frustratingly difficult to track the results of our activities. In my experience, that's one of the reasons that salespeople resist adopting social selling processes into their business. There isn't always a clear process with easily-defined steps leading to an easily-replicated ROI.

Just like prospects and customers are overwhelmed with the information and noise, so too are sales professionals. Just because we now have access to more prospects, and more information about these prospects, doesn't mean we have evolved a natural capacity to manage huge networks and leverage those relationships to create more sales. It might seem overwhelming, but we can indeed build up a core of best practices in the digital landscape. There are new technologies that help us manage the larger amounts of information that are now available. It's critical to learn how to effectively use these technologies to drive our sales process.

At its core, social selling is about using technology as a force multiplier. With this in mind, the first strategic step when using social selling is to examine which areas of the sales process are ripe for improvement. This will vary depending on your industry, sales cycle, experience, personality, and a host of other factors. A 30-year sales veteran who sells multi-year, multi-million dollar computer hardware packages will use social selling to fill different roles than a young saleswoman selling online advertising to small businesses.

> **At its core, social selling is about using technology as a force multiplier.**

This is not a "one-size-fits-all" process. Beyond the basics of a robust online presence, how you use social will depend on where you would focus your time without social. If you're on the "hunter" end of the spectrum wanting to develop a big funnel, social platforms give you access to huge numbers of people, along with a lot of data on them. You can use these tools to entrench yourself in social networks and build stronger reputations within them.

If instead you're a farmer working with a few named accounts, you can use online tools to research and get useful business intelligence about what's happening with those key prospects and customers. If your business grows by referrals, then using these tools to find out who your existing clients are connected to can be a valuable use of your time. If your product or service is most appropriate for a specific customer situation, you can monitor social media newsfeeds to be aware of when that situation is happening. There are many possibilities, so it's important to be intentional with your strategy.

The great thing about social selling and digital communication is they can be harnessed at all points of the selling process. Technology complicates the linear sales process, but it also opens up new ways to approach the business of finding, engaging, and selling to new prospects. Think about how these technologies have altered the prospecting phase alone. The wealth of information available online goes a long way to making sales prospecting more effective and efficient. Not only are there myriad ways to research the potential customer base, but there are many ways to manage this information more effectively once you have it.

The success of Salesforce.com over the past decade is demonstrative of the huge advantages that come from bringing technology to bear on the sales process. And using search tools on platforms like Twitter can let you know who is talking about your field, industry, or product. This ability to create targeted lists takes a lot of wasted effort out of the sales process. And in today's world, this efficiency is critical.

Along the same lines, the process of qualifying leads is now more efficient. We no longer go into conversations blind. Back when I sold cutlery in people's kitchens, there was a general rule of thumb that you could find out a lot about a person by what was on their refrigerator. Did they have a lot of pictures of the family, or was it a bunch of takeout menus? Today's qualifying process is a whole lot more nuanced, to say the least.

The Sales Sherpas of the digital era need platforms where they can offer their guidance and demonstrate their expertise. They need to position themselves as the guides their buyers need and want. Online sites are a treasure trove of tools that salespeople can use to consistently communicate to their network, and it's more important than ever to know how to use these tools wisely.

Conclusion

Mastering Sales Today to Succeed Tomorrow

Technology is truly providing us with amazing new tools. When I want to schedule a meeting with my friend Andy Crestodina, for example, I send a message to his assistant, Amy. Having an assistant helps Andy a lot. He runs a 30-person marketing firm, writes constantly (he wrote the best-selling *Content Chemistry*), and is a highly-sought speaker on the conference circuit. Amy looks at his existing appointments and finds a place to fit me in. We correspond back and forth until we find something that works for both of us. It's easy and relatively painless. She's a great assistant who frees up a lot of time and attention for Andy.

Amy is also an AI program.[74]

So what does that mean for the future of business? Are we eventually going to have a bunch of AI programs talking to each other? Going back to one of the movies we mentioned earlier, will we eventually be living in pods while computer programs control our realities, like in *The Matrix*? Will *everything* be automated? Lately, there's a lot of chatter about software that can write pop songs and poetry. If that's the case, they will eventually automate the entire sales process...right? Whether it's tomorrow, next year, or in the next decade, maybe all of us sales professionals will be on the streets, looking for something to do.

This sounds pretty dire, but I don't think we need to worry. When we first looked at the evolution of sales in Part I, I talked about the four As that the sales world has been trying to fill during the past 200 years: Availability, Awareness, Appreciation, and Attention. Sales has always tried to fill a gap, a lack of something. That something, however, has changed throughout the years. As we have

> As it turns out, being a Sales Sherpa isn't always easy, and that's fantastic news for the sales profession. It means we're not about to become extinct, no matter how many poetry-composing AIs there are.

seen, the digital age has made things both easier and harder for both buyers and sellers—there is an overabundance of information, and it's become difficult to distinguish the valuable signal from the background noise. In a world where time and attention are at a premium, the successful sales rep must position themselves as a Sales Sherpa working in the complex landscape of the Sales Matrix. As it turns out, being a Sales Sherpa isn't always easy, and that's fantastic news for the sales profession. It means we're not about to become extinct, no matter how many poetry-composing AIs there are.

As we come to a close, I hope you'll indulge my brief speculation on the next phase in the evolution of sales. When we look at the changes in technology that continue to move at breakneck speeds, we see a world where many of the tasks currently driven by people can and will be taken over by computers. As I write this sentence, advanced buyer algorithms are being created for big data analysis. Marketing automation is being driven by AI programs that know exactly who to approach, and when. Robo-advisors in financial services and other industries are giving financial, career, or even personal advice based on past patterns. And I'm sure there are a host of other applications that haven't even been invented yet, but will quickly become an irreplaceable part of our lives.

This seems to indicate that the sales role will fight the good fight for a while, and then slowly (or not slowly) continue its journey into obsolescence. But personally, I'm not so sure. Right now, sales professionals are working within an extraordinarily valuable niche that has come into its own very recently. This niche is what I have discussed at length: that of the Sales Sherpa. This role really does bring incredible value to our clients. Eventually, though, aspects of this role might not be as important as they are today. Sherpas help prospects decipher the dizzying array of information available online, but it's feasible that computer programs will eventually help with this task. If that happens, salespeople will have to find a new niche. And I think that at core, the role of tomorrow's salesperson will always hinge on one thing: Trust.

> As technology becomes more prevalent in our lives, it's becoming more and more important that we're able to trust the people we work with, because we know that the algorithms don't always have our best interests in mind.

No matter how accurate today's algorithms have become, we don't exactly trust them, do we? You can see this with our distrust of the algorithms that guide social media newsfeeds. My wife and I can have the same people in our Facebook networks, yet receive totally different updates. It's been shown that two people can have totally different results from the same Google search based on the same word,[75] and we can't really know why, because Google's algorithm is proprietary—it's a corporate secret. As technology becomes more prevalent in our lives, it's becoming more and more important that we're able to trust the people we work with, because we know that the algorithms don't always have our best interests in mind.

Technology has evolved vastly in the last couple hundred years, but people haven't, and we still value trust above almost any other quality. It's important to remember that for all of its power of analysis and prediction, the digital world hasn't been able to capture the interpersonal skills that even a child has. Humans are still important to other humans. Our interactions are incredibly complex, and trust can't be boiled down to a set of equations that we can put into a bot on our company's website.

At the same time, sales professionals are working in a larger context of distrust in the world around them. The 2017 Edelman Trust Barometer was entitled "Trust in Crisis" because in the year 2016, each of the major institutional trust measurements that it tracks took huge hits.[76] Today, people are much less likely to trust the organizations and institutions in their lives, and that vacuum is going to be filled by putting their trust into individuals. And as the Trust Barometer showed, the people we want to place our trust with aren't leaders, CEOs, or renowned experts. It is our peers—in the Trust Barometer study, it was other employees. *This* is the gap that salespeople are going to continue to fill. They can create trust in a way that a robot or a faceless organization can't.

> The salesperson who understands the importance of trust will be very well-positioned for the future.

The salesperson who understands the importance of trust will be very well-positioned for the future. When we look at the evolution of sales, it's easy to put a flag in the sand and describe how things are now. That's what this book has tried to do. But as we saw in Chapter 1, it's a mistake to think that we live in a static world. It will keep changing and evolving, just like it always has. It's important to understand and develop the capabilities and capacities that create success for today, because they're different than the ones from yesterday. But we also have to prepare ourselves for the world of tomorrow, because it's going to come quickly.

The pace of change has heightened, and the "tomorrow" that we talk about isn't some theoretical world on the horizon, but a day that's rapidly approaching. In fact, tomorrow might not be a metaphor at all. The next big change might be waiting for you tomorrow morning when you show up to work. You'll have to rethink everything all over again in order to create the success you want. And if there's one thing you take away from this book, I hope it's the willingness to accept change and tackle the new challenges that each day brings. I wish you the best of luck with your Hyper-Connected selling, both today and tomorrow.

About the Author

David J.P. Fisher lives in Evanston, Illinois, next to a beautiful cemetery, which acts as a reminder every morning to not take life for granted (and to be on the lookout for zombies). He is an entrepreneur, coach, salesman, writer, meditator, marketer, musician, podcaster, son, friend, brother, slam poet, comedian, salsa dancer, lover of life, teller of bad jokes, yoga enthusiast, and an average cook—as long as it's pancakes, hummus, or a recent addition: pozole soup.

Known as D. Fish to everyone (except his mom and his wife), he is a sought-after speaker, author, and business coach. His first full-length book, ***Networking in the 21st Century: Why Your Network Sucks and What to Do About It,*** and its companion book series, have all been best-sellers. His passion for growth and development has allowed him to influence thousands of others during his professional career. As the president of RockStar Consulting, he helps individuals become RockStars both offline and online by building their networking, sales, and entrepreneurial skills.

Contact David

To get the latest updates and resources to become a Sales Sherpa in your career, visit:

HyperConnectedSelling.com

Hire David to speak to your organization:
If you are looking for a speaker for your next conference, sales-kickoff meeting, or association convention, have David share the power of Hyper-Connected Selling with your audience. He can deliver keynote, half-day, and full-day messages depending on your needs. To find out more, visit

davidjpfisher.com/speaking

Let people know what you think:
If you enjoyed this book and found it useful, head over to its page on Amazon and leave a review. The more positive reviews it has, the easier it is to get found by others looking to improve their sales career.

You can also find David online at all the usual places:

Blog: www.davidjpfisher.com
LinkedIn: www.linkedin.com/in/iamdfish
Twitter: @dfishrockstar

Thank You

When you get past your first books (I'm at lucky #7 now), you feel kind of weird thanking the same people over and over... But then I realized that it's the people that keep putting up with my crap that deserve continuous thanks, so I guess it's not so odd.

It's easy to think that the outside world pauses when you're writing a book, but that's rarely the case. In my life, the woman who was my girlfriend became my wife during the writing of this book. So she had to listen to me complain about writer's block and the price of wedding flowers all while we were putting together seating charts and music set lists. For all of that and more, I'm lucky to have such a demanding flower.

I connected with Katherine Don through a series of networking connections and reconnections, and she's been an amazing editorial partner from the start. Her first review of the manuscript had one paragraph patting me on the back and 9 pages telling me what to fix. She did it in such a nice way that I didn't even notice. (It helped that she was spot on about everything.) And then she took all of the pieces and put them together in a way that made sense.

Jane Atkinson coached me through the stress-inducing process of changing direction in my business after more than a decade. But she was on the money when her first question to me was, "Why aren't you telling more people how to sell, that's what you know better than just about anybody else?" Her insights find the right balance of challenging and affirming and this book is only here because of her guidance.

171

After seven books together, I'm not even surprised by the amazing work that Chris, Debbie, and the JetLaunch team bring to the design of my books. They just knock it out of the park every time. It's awesome to not even have to worry about it.

My parents and siblings continue to both support and tease me in a way that only family can do. But I wouldn't trade them for anything. And now I have in-laws, which contrary to most jokes, are amazing people. Thank you for allowing your daughter to marry me ☺.

My friends continue to be a wonderful source of support. Writing books can be a lonely process because it's just you and a computer screen (often at very odd hours). It's nice to have people ask me how the book is coming, even if my response is usually a sigh and a headshake. So thank you Chrissie, Colette, Amy, Rob, Ian, Brian, Joe, and Andy and everyone else.

I've been fortunate to bring a wide range of really smart people into my business world. I love getting to talk shop with them—these conversations are actually where a lot of the "aha" moments in my professional world come from. Any list would certainly lead to me forgetting someone, but I can at least include Andy Crestodina, Amy Heiss, Gretchen Halle, Sean Carey, Joey Davenport, Blane Warrene, Jenny Newman, Bernie Borges, Ryan Rhoten, Shane Purnell, Saul Marquez, Pat Helmers, Michelle Mazur, Gini Dietrich, Adam Stock, and Mike Muriel. If you don't see your name here and we've had a conversation in the last year about selling, social media, networking, entrepreneurship, or communication, just know that you should totally be on this list too.

And finally, though it sounds cliché, thank you for spending some time with me in these pages. In a book that points out the amazing demands that we now have on our time and attention, I'm humbled that you were willing to share some of yours with me. I am well aware of the gift, and I hope that I was able to give you something to think about while you were here.

Build a Stronger Network

Do you want to dive even deeper into
professional relationship building?

Check out the ***Networking in the 21st Century*** series:

Networking in the 21st Century: Why Your Network Sucks and What to Do About It

Networking in the 21st Century... For Sales Professionals

Networking in the 21st Century... On LinkedIn

Networking in the 21st Century... For Solopreneurs and Freelancers

Networking in the 21st Century... Within Your Company

Networking in the 21st Century... For Millennials

Available in Paperback, E-Book, and Audiobook
amazon.com/author/davidjpfisher

Endnotes

1 *Cisco's Visual Networking Index Initiative* available at http://www.cisco.com/c/en/us/solutions/collateral/service-provider/visual-networking-index-vni/vni-hyperconnectivity-wp.html

2 Bryan Kramer, *There Is No B2B or B2C: It's Human to Human #H2H* (PureMatter, 2014)

3 Max Roser and Esteban Ortiz-Ospina, *"Literacy"* (2016) *available at http://OurWorldInData.org*

4 *Facebook Company Info* available at http://newsroom.fb.com/company-info/

5 *"Selling Power 500 Largest Sales Forces"* (Selling Power Magazine, 2016) available at http://www.sellingpower.com/content/article/index.php?a=10545/selling-power-500/largest-sales-forces/2016

6 Personal search on LinkedIn, Dec 2016

7 *"Selling Power 500 Largest Sales Forces"* (Selling Power Magazine, 2016) available at http://www.sellingpower.com/content/article/index.php?a=10545/selling-power-500/largest-sales-forces/2016

8 Peter Thiel, *Zero to One: Notes on Startups, or How to Build the Future* (Crown Business, 2014)

9 Company history available at https://www.fuller.com/our-story/

10 *Door to Door* (TNT Originals, 2002)

11 Arthur C. Clarke, *Rendezvous with Rama* (Spectra, 1990)

12 U.S. Department of Health and Human Services National Center for Health Statistics

13   Dag Spicer, *"If You Can't Stand the Coding, Stay Out of the Kitchen: Three Chapters in the History of Home Automation"* (August, 2000) available at http://www.drdobbs.com/architecture-and-design/if-you-cant-stand-the-coding-stay-out-of/184404040

14   George J. Olszewski, *A History of the Washington Monument 1844-1968 Washington, D.C.* (1971) available at https://www.nps.gov/parkhistory/online_books/wamo/history/index.htm

15   Lydia Saad, *The "40-Hour" Workweek Is Actually Longer -- by Seven Hours* available at http://www.gallup.com/poll/175286/hour-workweek-actually-longer-seven-hours.aspx and Gallup's 2014 Work and Education Survey

16   Daniel Pink, *To Sell is Human* (Riverhead Books, 2012)

17   Jeffrey R. Brown and Austan Goolsbee, *Does the Internet Make Markets More Competitive? Evidence from the Life Insurance Industry* (2000) available at http://faculty.chicagobooth.edu/austan.goolsbee/research/insure.pdf

18   Sheena Iyengar, *The Art of Choosing (*Twelve Press, 2011)

19   Sharon Begley, *"The Science of Making Decisions"* (Newsweek, February 2011) available at http://www.newsweek.com/science-making-decisions-68627

20   Malcolm Gladwell, *Blink: The Power of Thinking Without Thinking* (Back Bay Book, 2007)

21   Ibid.

22   CEB Sales Executive Council Report (2011)

23   *How to Make Your Number in 2014* (Sales Benchmark Index, July 2013)

24   Kathleen Schaub, *"Social Buying Meets Social Selling: How Trusted Networks Improve the Purchase Experience"* (IDC, April 2014)

25   Mary Shea, *"The B2B Sales Force Digital Reboot"* (Forrester Research, Inc., October, 2015)

26   Mona Chalabi, *"How Many Times Does The Average Person Move?"* (January, 2015) available at https://fivethirtyeight.com/datalab/how-many-times-the-average-person-moves/

27   2016 National Association of REALTORS® Profile of Home Buyers and Sellers

28   Bureau of Labor Statistics report available at https://www.bls.gov/ooh/sales/real-estate-brokers-and-sales-agents.htm

29   Hank Barnes, *"Tech Go-to-Market: Sales Organizations Need to Upgrade Skills and Processes to Meet Buyer Expectations"* (Gartner Group, 2013) available at https://www.gartner.com/doc/2583516/tech-gotomarket-sales-organizations-need

30 *The 2016 B2B Buyer's Survey Report* (DemandGen, 2016) available at http://www.demandgenreport.com/resources/research/2016-b2b-buyer-s-survey-report

31 Hank Barnes, *"Beyond the Buying Cycle"* (Gartner 2016) available at http://blogs.gartner.com/hank-barnes/2016/03/29/beyond-the-buying-cycle/

32 *Sales Perception Survey*, (Hubspot, 2016)

33 Bridge Group *2015 SaaS Inside Sales Survey Report* available at http://www.forentrepreneurs.com/bridge-group-2015/

34 Encyclopedia.com available at http://www.encyclopedia.com/places/asia/nepal-and-bhutan-political-geography/sherpa

35 Nassim Nicholas Taleb, *Fooled by Randomness: The Hidden Role of Chance in Life and in the Markets* (Random House Trade Paperbacks, 2005)

36 Kathleen Schaub, *"Social Buying Meets Social Selling: How Trusted Networks Improve the Purchase Experience"* (IDC, April 2014)

37 *The 2016 B2B Buyer's Survey Report* (DemandGen, 2016) available at http://www.demandgenreport.com/resources/research/2016-b2b-buyer-s-survey-report

38 Greg J. Stephens, Lauren J. Silbert, and Uri Hasson, *"Speaker–listener neural coupling underlies successful communication"* (National Academy of the Science of the United States, April, 2010) available at http://www.pnas.org/content/107/32/14425.abstract

39 Good places to start would be Dan Ariely, *Predictably Irrational, Revised and Expanded Edition: The Hidden Forces That Shape Our Decisions* (Harper Perennial, 2010) or Daniel Kahneman, *Thinking, Fast and Slow* (Farrar, Straus and Giroux, 2011)

40 David Epstein, *The Sports Gene: Inside the Science of Extraordinary Athletic Performance* (Current, 2014) and TED talk *"Are athletes really getting faster, better, stronger?"* available at https://youtu.be/8COaMKbNrX0

41 Rachel Botsman, TED talk *"The currency of the new economy is trust"* available at https://youtu.be/kTqgiF4HmgQ

42 Mimi An and Emma Brudner, *State of Inbound 2015* (Hubspot, 2016) available at http://www.stateofinbound.com/

43 Dale Carnegie, *How to Win Friends and Influence People* (reprint Pocket, 1998)

44 Sherry Turkle, *Reclaiming Conversation: The Power of Talk in a Digital Age* (Penguin, 2015) and *Alone Together: Why We Expect More from Technology and Less from Each **Other*** (Basic Books, 2012)

45 Patricia Ryan Madson, *Don't Prepare, Just Show Up* (Bell Tower 2005)

46 Sarah Thurber and Dorte Nielsen, *The Secret of the Highly Creative Thinker: How to Make Connections Others Don't* (BIS Publishers, 2016)

47 Nassim Nicholas Taleb, *Fooled by Randomness: The Hidden Role of Chance in Life and in the Markets* (Random House Trade Paperbacks, 2005)

48 Andy Hoar, *Death of a (B2B) Salesman* (Forrester Research Inc., April 2015)

49 Brian Hilliard, David Alexander, and Ivan Misner, *Networking Like a Pro: Turning Contacts Into Connections* (Entrepreneur Press, 2010)

50 Sales Benchmark Index, *"How to Make Your Number in 2014"* (July 2013)

51 Charlene Li, *The Transformation of Selling: How Digital Enables Seamless Selling* (Altimeter, 2017) available at http://www2.prophet.com/Transformation-of-Selling

52 Ronald S. Burt, *Brokerage and Closure: An Introduction to Social Capital* (Oxford University Press, 2007)

53 Kurt Badenhausen, "Michael Jordan, David Beckham Lead the Highest-Paid Retired Athletes 2016" available at https://www.forbes.com/sites/kurtbadenhausen/2016/03/30/the-highest-paid-retired-athletes-2016/

54 Ryan Rhoten, *CareerKred - 4 Simple Steps to Build Your Digital Brand and Boost Dredibility in Your Career* (Hybrid Global Publishing, 2017)

55 Vince Lombardi, *"What it takes to be #1"* available at http://www.vince-lombardi.com/number-one.html

56 Frank Newport *"The New Era of Communication Among Americans"* (Gallup, November 2014) available at http://www.gallup.com/poll/179288/new-era-communication-americans.aspx

57 Internet Live Stats (March, 2017) available at http://www.internetlivestats.com/one-second/#email-band

58 Dale Lampertz, *Has Cold Calling Gone Cold* (Keller Research Center, September 2012) available at https://www.baylor.edu/content/services/document.php/183060.pdf

59 Kathleen Schaub, *"Social Buying Meets Social Selling: How Trusted Networks Improve the Purchase Experience"* (IDC, April 2014)

60 *What happens online in 60 seconds?* (SmartInsights.com, Feb 2017) available at http://www.smartinsights.com/internet-marketing-statistics/happens-online-60-seconds/

61 *Internetlivestats.com* available at http://www.internetlivestats.com/total-number-of-websites/

62 Ryan Rhoten, *CareerKred - 4 Simple Steps to Build Your Digital Brand and Boost Credibility in Your Career* (Hybrid Global Publishing, 2017)

63 David M. Levy, *Mindful Tech: How to Bring Balance to Our Digital Lives* (Yale University Press, 2016)

64 Heather Wadlinger Ph.D., *B2B Report Millennials* (Sacunas, 2016) available at http://sacunas.net/reports/Millennial-B2B-Report_Sacunas-web.pdf

65 Aaron Smith and Monica Anderson, "*5 facts about online dating*" (Pew Research, February 2016) available at http://www.pewresearch.org/fact-tank/2016/02/29/5-facts-about-online-dating/

66 Meredith Broussard, "*Dating statistics you should know*" (Match.com) available at http://www.match.com/magazine/article/4671/

67 "*Garnering Traffic through Google*" available at http://www.mr-seo.com/seo-articles/importance-first-page-rankings/

68 Jeff Bullas, "*Why You should Forget about LinkedIn*" (April 2015) available at http://www.jeffbullas.com/2016/04/15/why-you-should-forget-about-linkedin/

69 Michael Drout, *The Modern Scholar: Way with Words: Writing Rhetoric and the Art of Persuasion* (Recorded Books, 2008)

70 Piyush Mangukiya, *Social Media by the Numbers* (Huffington Post, April 2016) available at http://www.huffingtonpost.com/piyush-man-gukiya/social-media-by-the-numbe_b_9757926.html

71 Mark Granovetter, *The Strength of Weak Ties* (American Journal of Sociology, May 1973) available at https://sociology.stanford.edu/sites/default/files/publications/the_strength_of_weak_ties_and_exch_w-gans.pdf

72 Will Barron, "*From Network Zero to Networking Hero*" (The Salesman Podcast, 2016) available at *https://www.youtube.com/watch?v=xxv7GdB3K0g*

73 Jack Kosakowski, available at http://www.jackkosakowski.com/

74 Available at https://x.ai/

75 Eli Pariser, "*Beware Online Filter Bubbles*" available at https://www.ted.com/talks/eli_pariser_beware_online_filter_bubbles

76 *2017 Edelmen Trust Barometer* available at http://www.edelman.com/global-results/